YEL
PI.

COMMIE LOVERS

A SYNOPSIS OF EVENTS
that show how much more
VULNERABLE AMERICA
Has Become to a Foreign TAKEOVER
THRU an INTERNAL SOURCE that -
this close to an Important Election -
shows all too clearly, the signs of
being able to destroy OUR Democracy!
SIGNIFICANT EARLIER WRITERS
also show how this process can
TAKE a DEMOCRACY to FASCISM
in a 4 year process that is hidden by
the LIES that CONCEAL it till it is
WAY TOO LATE to REVERSE!!
BY
MOSWEE M. PEACH

DIRECTOR BOOK PRESS

Printed in the United States of America

Published by: Director Book Press
USA

Library of Congress Cataloging - in - Publication Data
America DIES when Stump LIES, Moscow, Pyongyang, Black Lives
Resident, OVID 19, virus, Pandemic, HOAX, 2020 Election,
Bounty on American Soldiers, Taliban, Putin, Federal Troops
HOW to *FAKE* AMERICA GREAT AGAIN

A book by: DIRECTOR BOOK PRESS
ISBN 979 - 8 - 68186 - 258 - 1
First printing September 2020

TABLE OF CONTENTS

This book is an absolute must read to discover what has happened in the past almost totally disastrous three plus years. I've read books written some years ago that talked about roles played when the GOP occupied the White House before. Those seemed to be just as dramatically bad. That it could be worse - much worse - even in the bad GOP years 8 years ago - the people in charge actually believed in the rule of law, the Constitution, the institutions and the traditions that make up the Democratic government of the United States.

What we have run into here is apparently a person that may have never read the Constitution or may have no interest in it and may feel that he is the United States of America. Anything he says or does 'is' what the United States of America is or does. He seems to think that three equal branches with powers of checks and balances to regulate the other two branches is meaningless. Just because the Constitution, laws and regulations may say that he must do certain things - somewhere he seems to have it in his head, that's all actually irrelevant - If he just decides that he doesn't want to do it. The bottom line is: who the hell is going to stop him for not doing it? Well, you will see as you go through this book what a dilemma this has turned out to be. And, by far, - it is not over!

A goal of this book is to bring a broader awareness of what has been going on to a larger spectrum of the population so that perhaps, from that, appropriate actions, such as using our last meaningful opportunity to rid this great nation of a bad cancer may be taken. This fall vote is as crucial as the American Revolutionary war was to eventually turn this Nation around and get us aimed at a much better place. God help! We need all you can do to rid us of these 2 cancerous Pandemics.

YELLOW - PINKO COMMIE LOVER

We had a phrase in the 60's - 80's that was very much a Republican term. It was a constant Mantra of the Republicans. So much so that we couldn't escape it on a daily basis. It was so prominent that when I was consulting in DC and driving from Pennsylvania to Alexandria Virginia - before crossing the bridge over to Virginia - there was a sign posted on a scrub tree next to the river that said "Goddamn F----ing Pinko Commie Lovers"! Well, that's how prominent that sentiment was then being posted out in the wilderness on a crude sign board. Presumably it might still be one today because the relationship with Russia - if anything - has become more aggressive under its current leader. It seems his declared intent is to dismantle the power and influence of the United States in the entire world. In addition they seem to basically be trying to interrupt our ability to govern effectively. In fact, they might be considered one of our most serious, dangerous adversaries - that the United States has faced in decades.

Why do I bring this up now after so many years? Because the history which we all knew - Democrats and Republicans - that seemed so appropriate at the time has been obliterated. We seemingly forgot who our common adversary was. We seem to forget how serious we as a nation took it to go to the extent of calling people who befriended or sympathized with Russia "Pinko Commie Lovers". That phrase, as damning and disgusting as it is, totally brings out the very strong emotions which show how much disgust we had for those who would consider being sympathetic or empathetic with Russia! So how did we get here? Damn it! It unfortunately simply took us too long to figure out what many of us seemed to know from

2   the start. For far too long there was not enough solid evidence to make it a legitimate concern. However, with the impeachment hearings and what we seem to know about an incident of trying to get the Ukraine to interfere with our election in favor of the Resident is epiphonal. We can now see back through the history we've known for 3 years. He seems, from far before the election, to be a russian puppet - a kind of manchurian candidate - even so today. His domestic and foreign actions seem consistent with carrying out Russia's playbook and wishes for the destruction of the United States.

Here is the damning part. Russia, a master of propagating lies, misinformation and conspiracy theories to divert attention from their dastardly deeds, seems totally successful at getting the Republicans to do their dirty work for them as well. The Republicans you say? The very ones who called them "Pinko Commies" just decades ago? What has happened? How can this be? How could the staunch GOP be corrupted so far as to seemingly love the "Pinko Commies" they so vehemently hated for so many decades?

Because the Republicans, perhaps having pledged loyalty to the Resident instead of the Constitution, seem ignorantly trying to defend their Resident by repeating re-branded Russian mis-information propaganda as the Gospel! Why? Because it serves the Resident's need for absolute loyalty against impeachment? As a result, the top of the Republican Party is seemingly doing Russia's dirty work for them. No, not just very gladly but seemingly happy doing it! These are the same people who only decades ago were calling anybody who was befriending Russia - "Pinko Commie Lovers". How very far we have fallen as a nation! How very close we seem to becoming a nationlist authoritarian nation where "the rule of law" seems meaningless and the justice department seems to be working against the needs of the people of the United States. Hopefully, not forever. May God please help us!

It would appear we now have the Republican party's new title of "Pinko Commie Lover - Lovers" by their fealty to this Resident. So much so that they seem to do his bidding and by so doing have become "Pinko Commie Lover" -- Lovers. They seem blindly mesmerized by his commitments, phrases and ways to the extent that they seem willing to do the dirty work of a foreign adversary - Russia. Putin must be laughing his ass off! If this is so, it has the United States committed to a degree of destruction far beyond his wildest dreams - even far greater than his grossest expectations. We need only to look back into the past to see a path that might have brought them to this low point in their existence.

How did we let ourselves get here? By what total insanity did we allow a Resident to be selected that could do so much irreversible destruction of core values, beloved institutions and honorable standing in the world and with our allies? Oh yes, apparently we didn't! Was it not Russia who secretly, thoroughly attacked our election?! Is it not now seemingly apparent that this Resident may have been selected by an overwhelmingly effective election interference? It might be shown, if not certain, that the then hidden but now known interference from Russia might have been a huge factor in this horrendous outcome of the 2016 selection!

There were over 100 direct contacts by high level members of the Resident's campaign with high level contacts in the Russian hierarchy during the campaign. Almost all, if not all, of them denied this at least once before they all admitted it when confronted with evidence. How many times did Simon Peter deny knowing Christ before the rooster crowed?

4   What was there to hide if such contacts were up and up and above board? Nothing! Only people caught doing something that is not allowed would attempt to conceal it so ineptly though consistently, so predictably! What kind of mind warp might allow normally sane and reasonably thinking people - people who previously seemingly had a conscience, a moral compass, a reputation - to be suckered into doing something illegal, immoral, insane - things to select a terribly flawed, inept, ego driven, insanely narcissistic individual to the White House? What was in it for them to completely sell their souls and reputations? The souls sold so cheaply for pennies which cannot ever be recovered for even millions upon millions - at no price - whatever! These were followed by people who are like graham crackers, oil barons, river jordans, and a not so newness - and so on and on as it goes.

Have any of these people ever watched recent recordings of themselves on TV? Do they not see how totally diminutive they now appear compared to their former selves? Would they not find their present actions and rantings to be totally repugnant to their former persons of worthy standings? And for what? 30 pieces of silver? Selling one's soul for any price is the very definition of Nether. 'Nether' here nor there. Nether Definition: Soulless - is without reason for being or purpose.

This epiphany came to me in a dream. A dream so completely scary that I awoke in a total fright! Dreams, I don't remember. I think they are fantastic but the minute I wake up they're gone. This one was exceptional. I remembered it completely. What my mind so vividly captured in my psyche was a vision of how this great nation - these United States of America - the beacon of democracy, the leader of the Free World - could be taken over and now be apparently on a path to complete

destruction - seemingly engineered by the Soviet Union
perhaps through the means of a possibly egotistical puppet!

Knowing the Resident, it's conceivable that he could be flattered and manipulated into doing Putin's playbook. However, the scary part is that people who would normally step up and say to the Resident - 'You cannot do this! You must not do this! This is against the Constitution'! These very same people might have been mind warped and engineered to do Putin's bidding as well! If that happens, Heaven Help Us all! If there is no one nor a group of people who are normally Defenders of the Constitution who will step up and say 'this is not right, this cannot be, this has got to stop now' - then who will stop this madness of a possible march to destruction? If - when they refuse to do that - we would be totally screwed.

Those of us who lived through the Second World War - those of us who remember the very slow, incremental way that it progressed - step by step, freedom by freedom, - how the government was taken over and dominated by a nationalist dictatorship, remember well the signs that may already have occurred in the U S to the Democracy of the United States.

Let's start with the appointment of an Attorney General that seems loyal to the Resident more than to his oath of office to defend and protect the people of the United States or the Constitution. When you stack the Supreme Court with judges that seem loyal, not only to you but, to ideals contrary to the norms and mores of the entire nation, they not only seem to bow to the white house but seem willing to rule in favor of bizarre laws and processes contrary to the very core values, spirit and moral issues of the United States itself.

6   Hundreds of secondary courts have been stacked by very conservative judges - some of which have never been a judge or ever tried a case but seemingly support the Resident completely - apparently bending to ideals of this seemingly Nationalist leaning new form of government.

Having just watched a film of how the slow drip by drip of change - some small changes that might be noticed but could not be stopped - leading to larger changes that could not be stopped - and thus allowing Germany to become the fascist dictatorship under its leader - it is now scary to see what has happened in this nation in just the last two to six months.

Just consider the possible existence of a person who seems in charge of getting loyalty oaths from people appointed by the Resident or of people already in agencies or departments that might be asked to pledge their loyalty to the Resident instead of to the Rule of Law, the Constitution or the people of the United States. This could be a drip by drip step that may take us from the essence of a democracy, which we have all known and cherished, to the essence of a nationalist form of government. These Oaths just do not exist in Democracies!

For those who don't remember the Second World War - or were not alive at the time - surely remember Russia and now Russia under Putin and can visualize what life in that country must be under that kind of leadership. Loyalty oaths - except to the Constitution - are absolutely forbidden in a Democracy.

But who is going to stop this Resident? Nobody seems to be inclined to do that - at least not those who hold the power to do it. Apparently, they have all fallen under the spell of not only the Resident, but of a puppet master in Russia and thereby, may have all become Yellow - Pinko Commie Lovers.

How significant just one letter makes in this important phrase filed as a Trademark by Donald J. Trump on November 12th, 2012 just 6 days after Obama was re-elected for the second term. What does it mean when he claims he didn't decide to run until 2014 or 2015 when he came down the golden elevator in Trump Tower with his wife Melania?

Here is the proof that Donald J. Trump filed for the trademark "Make America Great Again" in November 2012 just six days after Obama won his second term. This fact goes against so many tales that the Resident has told about actions that were taken by Russia and that he had nothing to do with it because he had not even thought of running for president. This clearly shows when he started thinking about it and could be directly related to the date: - when he was running the Miss Universe pageant in Moscow in Russia on November 9, 2013.

He filed for this famous phrase - 'Make America Great Again' almost exactly a year before the pageant in Moscow in 2013. The connections to make the pageant possible were with Aras and Emin Agalarov - a Russian Real Estate Developer and his son - a Russian pop star singer. They purportedly paid Trump from 14 Million to 20 million dollars in support of the pageant near Moscow Russia in 2013.

A Tweet from: @AgalarovAras: I had a great weekend with you and your family. You have done a FANTASTIC job. TRUMP TOWER MOSCOW is next. Emin was WOW!

8   According to his publicist, Rob Goldstone, Emin requested the June 16th meeting between Donald Trump Jr. and Russian lawyer Natalia Veselnitskaya. Doesn't that seem a little bit too cozy for a coincidence? Trump apparently didn't meet Putin at the pageant but did meet with a number of oligarchs and was very happy about the prospects for a possible run for the President of the USA.

A post in the September 18th 2017 <u>The Guardian</u> indicates there were an awful lot of connections starting with those leading to the Miss Universe pageant in Russia near Moscow in 2013 and involving other oligarchs that were involved with Sberbank - Russia's largest bank; and money laundering and other such activities. See for example:

https://www.theguardian.com/us-news/2017/sep/18/trump-in-moscow-what-happened-at-miss-universe-in-2013

ColdStone's garbled billing for Yuri Chaika, the Russian prosecutor general - wanted the Trump campaign to have some documents that would 'incriminate Hillary', he said. And the Agalarovs would deliver them.

'This is obviously very high level and sensitive information but is part of Russia and its government's support for Mr. Trump - helped along by Aras and Emin,' Goldstone wrote. Rather than express surprise or question the apparent Kremlin operation Goldstone was describing, Donald Jr. pressed ahead and arranged the meeting. ('If that's what you say, I love it,' he replied In an email.)

Pulling the strings on the abortive deal (a Russian Moscow Trump Tower deal) was Felix Sater, yet another Russian business associate of Trump, who once served time in prison

stabbing a man in the face with a broken cocktail glass.   9
Sater reportedly told Trump's attorney in an email: 'I will get
Putin on this program and we will get Donald elected.' 'Buddy,
our boy can become President of the USA and we can
engineer it ... I will get all of Putin's team to buy in on this.'
 for
Printed in The Guardian July 16, 2018 is a reference:
Fresh off a controversial summit (in Helsinki) that drew
widespread condemnation from America and its allies,
Vladimer Putin and Donald Trump struck a defiant tone in a
pair of television interviews that sought to dismiss Russian
interference in the 2016 presidential election.

Hours after Trump's joint appearance with Putin in Helsinki, it
was dubbed by some US officials as 'treasonous' that the
Russian president rejected allegations that his government
meddled in the 2016 election and called them 'utterly
ridiculous'.

See for example:
https://www.theguardian.com/world/2018/jul/16/
vladimir-putin-denies-russia-election-meddling-us-
election-trump

10 Here is a copy of Trump's November 12, 2012 application for the "Make America Great Again" - Trademark

UNITED STATES PATENT AND TRADEMARK OFFICE
APPLICATION FOR REGISTRATION OF A TRADEMARK

MARK:	**MAKE AMERICA GREAT AGAIN**
CLASS:	35
APPLICANT:	Donald J. Trump
ADDRESS:	725 Fifth Avenue New York, NY 10022
ENTITY:	a United States citizen
OUR REF:	TRMP 1207224

The above-identified applicant has a bona fide intention to use the above mark in commerce on or in connection with the following services, and requests that said mark be registered in the United States Patent and Trademark Office on the Principal Register established by the Act of July 5, 1946 under Section 1(b):

Class	Services
35	Political action committee services, namely, promoting public awareness of political issues and fundraising in the field of politics

The mark is in standard characters and no claim is made to any particular font style, size or color.

Donald J. Trump

By: _____
[Signature]

Date: **11/12/12**

Note: the trademark was filed under the Class 35 which indicated it was for Political action committees services, promoting public awareness of political issues and fundraising in the field of politics.

IGNORANT
or in the south just plain IGNERT

It probably doesn't even need a page for the reader to know what this chapter is all about. Isn't it just so GD obvious?

When you have a person who is dealing with a worldwide pandemic of a brand new deadly viral disease and you're making political jabs about it in order to score political points against your perceived political opponents - you just might have come under this chapter heading. To call a Gold Star family names or to make remarks about judges who are actually overseeing a case in which you're involved or just calling adults diminutive names - I would think you just might fall totally under the Heading of this chapter.

We don't even have to go into the dictionary definition of the first word or the southern word because they are both there and can be found. The world, and I mean the world - must stand in dumbfounded awe that anybody, and particularly one of high stature, would emit anything like this about anybody or anything else. What comes out of the mouth of this person defies common sense, reasoning and good judgment. It does not justify any measure of sanity, nor can it justify any sense of being just a normal human. Where's the normality in this?

The words have nothing to do with education or book learning but have everything to do with just plain common sense and decency. 2000 years of recorded history have taught us many lessons about human behavior. And one thing that has been pretty effectively removed from human discourse, at least in high levels of human discourse, is this kind of behavior. Is this not so? Enough Said?! You pretty much get it and probably already know it! You're not Ignert.

CHAPTER 4
GARDEN PATH SYNDROME

Do you know when you're walking down a Garden Path and you come to a 'Y' and there's a decision to be made. Do I go left or go right? You know not what is ahead. You don't know whether it is a Rose Garden or a Chinese or Italian or classic French Garden. You don't know what is to be expected so you just make the most intelligent decision that you can based upon what you know at the moment. You make that decision and proceed either left or right. As you go, you are seeing lovely blooms and smelling the roses. After making quite a large number of steps you discover that you are now walking in a crummy area filled with weeds, wildflowers, thistles and other lesser things. Did I make the wrong choice?

I mean, you could go back, perhaps, and take the other path. Would that be better? 'Perhaps it will get better if I keep going 999 more steps' and this patch of wildness will dissipate and I will be in something marvelous like a Chinese Garden. Guess what? You've committed perhaps 1000 steps. It's a long way back to the 'Y' and it hasn't been all that bad. Yes, there are some drawbacks. Yes, it isn't exactly what your expectations were but now you're committed. It's quite a ways back so you decide to keep going. You've made a decision - seemingly wrong - but you hope that it could get better. That in essence is: "The Garden Path Syndrome".

How many times have we experienced that very same thing in our lives, business, relationships or dating people? Perhaps, if you spend a certain amount of time dedicated to a certain project or 'dating' a person of interest - you think 'hey OK'. 'It seems to be getting better'. 'I don't know when I'm going to get to what I really like about this person'. The things I need to know about this person are not coming forward. They're not springing forth immediately because it takes time to know if what you are looking for is true. As a result you keep going. In the meantime, had you started in the other direction with XY or Z, you may have gotten to where you wanted to go. You might have been satisfied by now.

Unfortunately, you've invested three or four months working in this direction. What you do is human nature. You've invested so much and things are seemingly getting better. 'I'm just not there yet.' 'Perhaps around the next corner.' Perhaps through the hedge into the next venue. Perhaps then, you will have that breakthrough. Guess what. You keep going. You invest another three months. Now, to go back, you have wasted six months. 'Oh my, had I gone back perhaps I would have met my goal but after 6 months I am nowhere.' Well perhaps it isn't that bad. Possibly, you can live with this? I think you are now getting the gist of what I am trying to say.

We ended up with somebody who, those who voted for him thought, would make: America <u>whatever</u> Again. And he did make America <u>whatever</u> Again. There's the problem. Those loyal followers must now have considerable doubts, having made this decision against considerable odds 'and won'. Looking back, to see that perhaps the opposition might be right in saying things like he seems to be a con man, a narcissist, a totally self-centered person could be a problem. When they made that decision there were a lot of people saying: 'You know, you've got to see the character, the lying, the cheating, the business dealings and the ego.' For those that shot their Silver Bullets - it's damn hard to admit they may've made a terrible mistake. 'What a horrible mistake I made.' 'Oh my God, this isn't right but I've got to stick to it.'

14   I've got to stick to it because otherwise, I have to tell all of my friends and people who chided me for my decision to take this path - 'Oh my God, I must be so wrong - so very wrong!' Do you know how hard that is for any person to do? It's Only Human Nature. Being what it is - it is almost impossible to go back to the 'Y' on the garden path. Damn it!

So guess what? We keep going down the same path and only a few decide to bail - to damn the torpedoes and say; 'I'm going to bail and go back and take a different path.' This is so typical behavior. I've seen it so many times. In business, a manager needs to shoot 5 silver bullets with his management to justify the expense of hiring a 'super duper person'. To hire this person - paying him an exorbitant salary - nobody else is being paid - to ship all his goods - boats, planes and cars at a huge cost and end up with someone that, within a month, everybody knows is a jerk and a total waste of time. A total idiot. Someone who just does not fit the organization but thinks he's 10+. Not only can't he do a damn thing, he is totally disruptive to the rest of the group. He destroys the unity, the dignity, the morale and he will eventually destroy the group.

You can't get the manager to listen to what you're saying. The manager, having shot the bullets will say; 'You just don't understand.' 'This person is good for us.' 'You will get used to him.' 'You'll see.' 'He will be good for us and our successes.' Bottom line: It just doesn't work out! It just never works out!

Bullshit! The group knew within 10 minutes that this person was totally disruptive, unproductive, a total mistake but the manager having shot his last five silver bullets, cannot admit the mistake to his management because - guess what? He, just might be fired for doing something so obviously stupid.

Well, I think you know what I'm talkin' about. I'm talking about where we are in this place right now with this dire situation. You are not going to convince that group of people that committed this "non function" to a position of power that they made a mistake. You have got to do something else. Something else has to be done to solve it.

To say; 'I'm sorry, you have got to go now.' 'I'm sorry this just isn't working out.' 'I'm sorry this is not how it's going to continue.' That may be the way that it's done in American corporations - 'you're fired'. No, apparently we do not have that well understood capitalist option in our Democracy. Our last shot, perhaps our only shot - seemingly, in a game with a terribly tilted playing field not in our favor - is to shoot our very own 5 super silver bullets - in an overwhelming election in November and just hope to God that some of those former, disgruntled supporters may, perhaps, just join in. JUST DO IT!
* * * *

It may not be the right place in this book, but the situation has gotten so much worse - so terribly scary - must be said now. For those not yet familiar with what's currently going on in our country but also in the entire world - see chapters 17 and 19 about the COVID 19 worldwide pandemic. Pages 17, 61, 71.

When a person in authority is presented with a total disaster and may not get it or understand it, he might be forgiven for dragging his feet out of ignorance. But once told - many times - if he continues to drag his feet for an extended, long time - there's something or someone else pulling his strings! Why, in our apparently civilized world, would any decent man be so seemingly disinterested in saving 10's of thousands of lives by not taking action that he may have in his ability to control? Totally illogical - definitely against all of humanity. What other country/person might be interested in America's misfortune?

CHAPTER 5
THE SNOWBALL SYNDROME EFFECT

Have you seen when a snowball rolls down a hill in fresh snow it will pick up snow as it rolls and get bigger and bigger as it goes? Well, that's the image I want you to keep in mind as we talk about this subject.

Picture a cartoon where a man is running for his life down a hillside with a snowball rolling behind him getting bigger and bigger the further they go. How many times have we seen this analogy in life and in business when a project manager has been reporting to his boss all along that everything is alright. 'Everything is perfect. Yes, we are on time and under budget. Everything's fine. Nothing to worry about'. Well, there are deadlines and benchmarks to projects and those deadlines have extreme significance and consequences. Must be met!

There are two kinds of managers. There's the one who does what I have just said and one who keeps his boss well informed and especially checks in early and often when there are difficult problems. With the first kind when the deadline hits, it's discovered that he's nowhere near finished, he's way over budget and he has multiple problems he has not told his boss about and doesn't know how to solve. That's when the snowball gets large enough that it rolls right over the man and crushes him. We can only hope that was always true.

Let's analyze this for a moment. What is the story here? The premise is when they lie - lie and lie continuously and use hyperbole to say how wonderful they've been and how much they've done and how great they are instead of telling us the truth right up front - that's the premise of the snowball effect syndrome in a nutshell. It depends on a "Crack" story!

When the Resident eliminated the pandemic task force two years ago it severely jeopardized our ability to quench a worldwide pandemic. These people studied animal viruses that might jump to humans. This was done to get a real jump start on any possible illness like the coronavirus that we are now facing. By taking this action he has set in motion the Perfect Storm for our current disaster. That is - not only being totally unprepared but not even having a clue of how to get a handle on how to prevent, mitigate or minimize the effect of this devastating, worldwide COVID19 pandemic.

That having been said - not only did they not jump in with both feet to quickly start solving this problem immediately - they instead, were worried about the negative image to the election, the ill effects to the stock market and all other negative consequences to his possible re-election that could be connected with the image of many people sick and dying. This was apparently far more important than starting an early, aggressive plan to slow and mitigate this dread disease and to minimize the effects on United States LIVES. Such action might just affirm that a huge disaster was coming - that might just be terrible news and images for the 2020 re-election.

The snowball effect has been propelled by multiple lies and exaggerations of what they have done, what they are doing and what tests will be available tomorrow or the next day. Unfortunately, if you are doing business with just people, you can probably tell lies and hyperbole over and over again and get by with it eventually. But when playing with people's lives, with something like a coronavirus that is a pandemic that is devastating the entire world and having horrendous numbers of the loss of life - that is a wholly different situation. I believe the snowball effect may just be about ready to occur. For the sake of all mankind, I hope not. It'll be very hard to survive.

18   We have had so many lies and hyperbole about how great they've been. Let's see; it was going to be a million tests. Oh that was last week. And they're not out this week? Now let me see. Was it 1 million, two million and now I hear it's 4 million tests by Wednesday? When was that supposed to be? Let me see the published talking points. Oh, sometime this week? Why have there been only perhaps 3000 tests performed weeks later? Why is it that even health professionals are not able to get tests performed?

Early widespread testing is a minimal requirement to pinpoint and understand the locations and dynamics of the start of a pandemic. Contact mapping is absolutely crucial. Otherwise, you are trying to find an invisible enemy in the dark without a flashlight or any sensor. High volume testing, like in South Korea, should have started at least by the end of January, '20.

Hey folks, this is real. There is absolutely no time for politics. This is Death about life. The economy is tanking - the people are in great fear and 10,000's of people are dying. This is no joke. How many tests have actually occurred? Perhaps only 1.3 million by April, 2020? Based on Lies - America dies!

Something just doesn't add up. Hey folks - People are dying all over the world! It's no time to promote dubious, not likely, conceptual drugs as healers. It's not just being criminal - it's a Crime against all of Humanity. Unlike a bogus Univ. this could very likely be a very, Deadly Hoax! People Die when Lied to! That's the Snowball Effect. Just about to roll over all of us!

I'm reminded of <u>The little Red Hen</u>. When begged for help the Feds were not in sight. But, when it was time to take the credit for work the states were forced to do, the Fed was first in line. States get to eat the CAKE . The Feds don't get a BITE!

HE IS an EMPTY VESSEL
Seemingly Into which has been poured Evil.

He seems to be an empty vessel into which someone poured evil magic and destructive practices to alter our very soul and strengths. Consequently, as a result, we may have lost our world influence, our institutions, our norms, our very being, our reliance on absolute truths, our form of government, our influence over others, our reputation, our allies, our existence based upon the Rule of Law, our way of life, our honor, our respect in the world, our beliefs and, the most disastrous result of all is: the loss of our international credibility. We can't be trusted. It seems our word abroad is not worth - Shit!

It must be so obvious, to all who observe, that Russia, with numerous think tanks and Military Intelligence organizations, has been studying the United States, its form of government and its institutions. They have been studying its laws and the way the Constitution doesn't work and what means seem to be available to enforce these laws. They seem to know what happens if these institutions/laws are not followed or obeyed.

Our democracy is built upon the Rule of Law and on the basis of a defence of the Constitution. Congressmen, Senators, the President, members of the executive branch, members of the Courts, Supreme Court, etc. have all taken an oath of office when they took their positions to abide by and to defend the Constitution of the United States. So what has been gained by the Russian's extensive scrutiny of our form of government is apparently an analysis of every loophole, crevice, blind seam and huge chasms so large that you could drive many trucks through. That would seem to allow public officers the viable option of ignoring the laws and Institutions with real impunity.

20   So what if you ignore an oath of office? What if you ignore the laws, rules or traditions? What then? If nothing happens, it may show up the weaknesses in our form of government and expose how poorly our democracy works and how it might be completely destroyed. Nicely done Bozo.

It is only when reasonable people are there to serve the public, Constitution, United States and the rule of law that the system has a reasonable chance to work as designed. When people, who believe in these things are there to serve, will respect what is required - to respect tradition and the Rule of Law - that our government works as well as the founders intended. How'd we get the wrong one? Only one bad choice!

Apparently what is missing and was not protected against in the framing of the constitution was an effective means to prevent these consequences. It wasn't believed that anyone would even consider running for office in order to destroy the Rule of Law or the Constitution. The Constitution has no teeth for punishment, no means of taking someone to trial for breaking these laws and no means for incarcerating them when it happens that somebody decides they are not going to obey their oath and just do whatever they like or what may be whispered in their ears by an aggressive foreign government.

We see what happens when they decide that it's best for them or perhaps a foreign country and they just reject their oath of office. What is normal is what is expected. Who's going to stop them when they break precedent, not do what's common sense and just do whatever they feel like? Where in the law or the Constitution does it say that if you do this the gendarmes, the military, the CIA or the FBI or someone is going to come pick you up and haul you off to jail? The Constitution doesn't have the means to do that. Apparently, that is what we are finding out in Spades. We are finding that out in Spades what is apparently in the playbook. We now know that the empty shell is apparently where the playbook has poured it's evil magic and the Empty Shell seems doing their dirty work on a daily basis. The worst part is he is getting by with it and going scott-free. There is apparently nothing that we can do to stop him - even with impeachment! There is much to do!

If we have people duped by the Russian propaganda that won't even do anything about it and if you try him he becomes immune because they dismiss it and now he's even bolder and even more he seems untouchable like wearing Teflon suits. During the trial, Putin must have been LAUGHING his HEAD OFF as he was seemingly WINNING very Bigly! Then there's nothing stopping him. Now the only thing that can stop him is a '20 election or the COVID19 virus.

* * * * * A new thought that is now very timely * * * * *

This can't go as it's so serious and perhaps criminal by it's unintended effects. In the 4/23/20 virus meeting there was a report by Bill Brian who leads the science and technology lab at DHS that investigates potentially dangerous substances such as the biology of the COVID 19 virus. He reported upon results of sunlight (UV light) and various disinfectants like bleach and alcohol on killing COVID 19 on non porous surfaces. The results seemed very promising. The Resident speculated that perhaps injecting some of these substances or something like that might be determined to be very effective. It's known that Ingesting bleach could be fatal. That prompted a huge flurry of people calling into health departments to see if they should inject or swallow bleach to kill the virus. Worse yet, apparently a Mark Grenon of Genesis II proposes the use of chlorine dioxide (branded as MMS) to cure the virus - and sent a letter to this effect to the White House just days before this pandemic task force presentation.

CHAPTER 7
WHO'S the PUPPET and WHO'S the MASTER?

An awful lot of us suspected from the beginning there was a really strong endearing connection between the Selectident and Russia. This has been shown over and over again when the Selectident seems to belittle the world leaders, our Allies, Congressmen and Senators, the Judges, Gold Star families, and Political Opponents, Etc. It doesn't matter who they are but the person he never ever ridicules - not once in over 3 years - or belittles or calls childhood nicknames - is Putin. Who in hell has who or whom by the proverbial Balls? Could it be - Satan? Who is the Puppet? Who is the Puppet Master?

Mueller's Russia investigation was so disappointing - it might have been just as effective if written by a room full of monkeys with typewriters and with a lot less waste of time and money. And by far more importantly it meant two plus years wasted waiting for its production only to have it be a complete flop. TWO important years lost and down the drain!

We had far more information from news media, reporters and news investigators that painted the entire picture very clearly. Much clearer than Mueller ever showed. If Mueller had just organized, compiled and reported what he could gather from news clippings he might have made a much more imperative and definitive report that could've been showing a very clear connection between the Selectident and Russia. The most disappointing part was he had a whole team of financial experts who knew taxes that could look at money laundering and bank transactions and he seemingly did zero - absolutely nothing to look at those taxes or bank records or any money laundering transactions that might have implicated this Selectident with a direct connection with Russia.

What should have been done is what detectives do on big storyboards, putting pictures, names, notes, evidence found and things said with strings between to make connections and to annotate them. In the first place it seems so clear that Russia - not the Selectident - may have done much to get him selected by the Electoral College. It was a total of only 70,000 votes in three states that got him selected by the Electoral College when Hillary won the general election by more than 3 million votes. Pennsylvania, Wisconsin and Michigan were the only three states that were needed to select the Resident.

A possible connection of the Selectident and Russia was the desire to build a hotel in Moscow, and to meet Putin at the Miss Universe Pageant and possibly other connections. His campaign apparently made over a hundred connections. All of them denied, initially, and then only admitted to when they were confronted with the truth. Then they said that there's nothing wrong with them - claiming they were legal. It seems so clear that even an idiot might understand they might be involved in it. I don't know how it is that every time it looks like he's about to be found out or detected, something comes up to deflect from the truth. Something or someone, seemily with outside connections, seems to protect the Teflon coated person - keeping other people from understanding the truth.

Perhaps we finally hit the one thing that might clear it up one way or the other when all good people's efforts to normalize this cancer that has infected our Nation for more than 3 years has failed time and time again. Now there may be something that may actually be God's intervention: known by the code name - COVID19. Viral Pandemics in a non immune world population can be totally apolitical sudden equalizers. Viruses don't read Tweets. May this virus be so helpful when needed!

CHAPTER 8
THE VISITS to see KIM JONG-UN and PUTIN
Who in their right mind would let him alone with Putin?

Perhaps some of you may have seen, read or remember the book/play called *The Firebugs*: A Morality play - A Play by Max Frisch. A quote from play; 'If they were really firebugs, do you think they wouldn't already have matches?'

Max Frisch wrote this book after World War II, about how his countrymen ignored the rise of the Reich until too late. It's given in a metaphor of an arsonist in the neighborhood who comes to live in a house of a certain Mr. Biedermann, who is so concerned about 'not appearing unlikable', he refuses to believe the new may be an arsonist. This is in spite of him reeking of gasoline, and storing gasoline in the Attic of Mr. Biedermann's house. The arsonist continues asking everyone where he can get gasoline, fuses, matches etc. But Mr. Biedermann is in denial, and so, as his home is filled with gasoline barrels, the arsonist asks him for matches - which Mr. Beidermann gives him in order to appease him, hoping that if he's nice to him, he won't set fire to his house.

Right off the bat, this is a story everyone should read and particularly at this time, because it in itself is a metaphor of the times we are experiencing here in the United States. But if you think about it, it is a moral that goes way beyond that to the title of this chapter in very subtle and yet direct ways.

From the campaign to the end of the election in 2016 and then beyond, things were discovered about many conversations from the campaign to high-level people in Russia about the campaign and about what they may have intended to do after the inauguration. Just the suspicion that arose from this new information might make anyone worried about a possible

direct connection between the candidate and Russia.
Having this suspicion of possible collusion, why would anyone in their right mind, either in the government or beyond, even consider letting the Resident meet directly with Putin, or for that matter Kim Jong-Un, in a private meeting with no recorders, witnesses and no one to report what was discussed? One would think that might be absolutely worse than giving the Firebugs matches with a house (the United States) filled with gasoline. In any sane mind, that would be considered an outright insanity. Possibly an absolute No-No.

I know that you are now asking the question; 'who is Mr. Biedermann'? Can you guess? Oh come on now. You must know. It's all of those lackeys, GOP sycophant, Pinko Commie Lover -- Lovers - that's who. They are traditionally the ones who should stop him. They could make it mandatory that there be witnesses with notes taken and published as is customary in a free Democratic Society. But, oh no, they don't want to offend anybody - certainly not the Resident-in-Chief. It is just absolutely, perfectly insane to let this inane kind of thing to happen. Where oh where have we lost our senses?

Now it's time to talk about something possibly more serious in these discussions with Putin or with Kim Jung-Un. First, there are probably congratulatory slaps, from Putin, on the back of the Resident about how great a job he's doing dealing with the United State's reputation, institutions and ability to act as a Democracy. What if he asked more serious questions of transactional processes about what and how to do what might be next? For example, to Kim, he might ask; 'how do you go about controlling an entire population of free thinkers that are used to having the advantages and benefits of a

26   Democracy like we have been used to for centuries?' 'What kind of steps would I be taking next to reducing these Freedom's and Liberal ways of living?' 'I know where I want to go and I know that you know how to get me there.' 'That is something that I don't know and very much need you to help me to understand with a sequence of steps and processes.'

The things that seem confusing to us in America - being used to the ways of being in a government by and for the People - we don't understand Putin's or Kim Jong-Un's playbook well enough. We can't believe there could be anyone who lives here, that might even consider the possibility that things that they do might lead to the destruction of it all, or even less so, to the advantage of a Foreign Adversarial Government.

I think a great deal of the confusion stems from the Resident - his personality may get in the way of understanding what may really be happening or of the understanding of the bottom line about where the real action may be actually coming from.

The biggest characteristic is: the man is a super narcissist and everything in the world and everything that happens is always about him. Having absolutely no empathy for anything or anyone adds to the confusion. Any situation or tragedy whatsoever, does not affect him personally nor emotionally or with any sympathy or feelings at all. A total blank - Nada!

The result is uncharacteristic reactions to events; statements of fact which may show his shortcomings or any situation which - of a desperate nature - he reacts only to make himself look better - in charge and superior to anyone who preceded him. Thus the true story of any foreign influence is totally disguised, obfuscated and obliterated by his behaviors. It may turn out that's what's known as a total cover to Reality!

THE OATH
The Impeachment Phase

OATH of the President of the UNITED STATES:
"I do solemnly swear (or affirm) that I will faithfully execute the office of President of the United States, and will to the best of my ability, preserve, protect and defend the Constitution of the United States"

OATH taken by the Senators when sworn in as new Senators:
"I do solemnly swear (or affirm) that I will support and defend the Constitution of the United States against all enemies, foreign and domestic; that I will bear true faith and allegiance to the same; that I take this obligation freely, without any mental reservation or purpose of evasion; and that I will well and faithfully discharge the duties of the office on which I am about to enter: so help me God."

OATH taken by Senators before the Impeachment trial starts:
"I solemnly swear (or affirm) that in all things appertaining to the trial of the impeachment of Donald John Trump, president of the United States, now pending, I will do impartial justice according to the Constitution and laws: so help me God."

IMPEACHMENT: is the process by which a legislative body levels charges against a government official. ... in the United States, for example, impeachment at the federal level is limited to those who may have committed "Treason, Bribery, or other high crimes and misdemeanors".

Well, isn't it interesting that both the Resident and the Senators must swear an **OATH** when they take office; to *preserve, protect, support or defend the Constitution* of the

28   United States. In the Resident's case, 'to the *best of his ability'* and the Senators' case, '*against all enemies foreign and domestic.*'

Additionally in the Senators case; 'that I will bear *true faith and allegiance to the same*'.

Now, in the case of impeachment of the president, they take an additional oath and that adds; I will do *impartial justice* according to the *Constitution and laws*: so help me God.

It seems to me that there's a lot of powerful stuff involved in these OATHs and particularly in the case of impeachment that the <u>Constitution</u> and <u>the rule of law</u> are extremely important to those positions. The fact that they are the *sole* reasons for those positions makes it absolutely necessary that they must protect and defend <u>the rule of law and the Constitution for our very survival</u>! However, in the case of impeachment they have to go further and swear that they must, 'provide *impartial Justice* according to the *Constitution and the laws.*'

Guess what? It's totally understood by the importance of the binding words of these Oaths that the <u>Constitution, and the rule of law are so very important</u> that they are the very basis and foundation of our democracy and therefore fundamental to the survival of this Union, this Republic, this Democratic Union that was formed by our founders when they wrote the Constitution. Everything breaks down if we do not follow <u>the Rule of Law</u> or the rules and bindings of the <u>Constitution</u>. If that happens, we end up with, not a democracy but a dictatorship; a king, a dictator, a monarch. That is definitely not what we are about nor what the United States of America is about. It is not what we have lived and loved for the past 240 years and it is definitely not what we intend to live for in the next two hundred and forty years!

Do you know what is the saddest, scariest part? It is that there is a whole group of people - a whole class of people - who should know the Constitution inside and out - should know the absolute value of the Rule of Law - the absolute value of precedent, tradition and established institutions and how they are the glue that holds the union together against all forces, foreign or domestic, and that would be the destruction of this Democracy of the United States of America - the very Democracy of our very sacred Union. Fini!

Where are these rascals who swear by God so casually - so callously - so cheaply, so recklessly, that they risk the very basis of all of OUR lives, our hopes, our dreams, our futures - yes - our very existence?! Have they no wives, no children or grandchildren, no aunts or uncles that they treasure and love to know, that they are so greedingly risking all of this - OUR lives and future? And for what? A Bozo, a clown, a charlatan?

They seemingly take it so lightly; laying squander to it so easily like it's play money that they do not really own. Has the value, the real meaning and true significance totally evacuated them? Are they not aware of the true disaster that will follow by abandoning these precepts? In short, have they totally lost the faculty of their senses and well being? In other words have they completely lost their <u>bloody minds</u>?

What kind of mindless zombies have they become? What is the true source of this devilish nonsense? How is it being disseminated and controlled? Where are the levers being pulled that have taken decent law-abiding, God fearing men to abandon all that they have learned; all that they know and all that they feel - and have thrown it all in the trash? Have they watched themselves in their videos? Have they looked in the mirror? Have they talked to themselves and asked 'who am I,

30   where did I come from, what happened to the person I used to know that lived in this body?'

I hate to say it, but I've not seen such a totally illogical transformation like this since the late 30's and early 40's. America, among others, commited to go to bail the rest of those people out. Who in the hell is going to bail us out? Do you know of anyone? God, I'm afraid there may be no one but that it is up to us, in complete desperation, to save ourselves!

I love the part of the president's OATH that says '*I will to the best of my ability*'. Based on what we've all seen so far, there cannot be much hope for that. In fact, there may be no ability whatsoever! And are we not counting upon him to have our best interests and our positive futures most at heart?

If we are not benefiting from his wisdom, somebody must be, because something or someone keeps him going despite everything that stands against all reason that he either has the ability or the inclination to drive to a good future for us. Who feet-drags in a deadly pandemic? After apprised of this - continues to foot drag determinedly? All those God-fearing Senators. Heaven Help Us - I don't know what God they may be praying to. Apparently, not to a good, benevolent God!

P.S. We've all known people who are just mean spirited. We've also known people that have been 'normal' most or all of their lives but due to a trauma, terrible events or situations have become mean spirited - for a day, a week or perhaps several months - but years, 3+ years? That is not consistent with human nature. In the midst of this pandemic when it's not advisable to be close - the Wisconsin GOP legislature and Supreme Court seemingly colluded that they must vote at the polls today! Mail in? Blocked by U.S. S.C. by a 5 to 4 vote!

C. C. C. C. C. C. C.
He Conceived, Cajoled, Cheated, Caught, Chastised, Covered UP
and Chortled
Capitulated? Not on your Life. NEVER!

It doesn't take a rocket scientist to figure out from those words in this sequence what I'm talking about here. You can pretty much figure out it is about the actions of the Resident regarding possible Extortion of the Ukraine government to aid in his re-election and leading to his impeachment. But, for the sake of the book, I will try to spell them out in brief detail for you, so you would really understand how bad; how sinister; these really were. I will show right up front how it broke a number of laws in the process. One of these laws, Bribery, is specifically spelled out in the Constitution as justifying Impeachment and removal from office.

These must not be forgiven nor mimimalized as the GOP sycophants are succeeding to accomplish! The breaking of these laws is extremely dangerous to the future of this Democracy, this Republic and this Constitutional form of government - not to mention our very near and far freedoms, liberties and the rule of law. All derived from the Constitution, spawned by our patriotic founders. All are involved in this.

CONCEIVED
The Resident apparently conceived this "Drug Deal" scheme as far back as May 2019 as a means to;

1. Use a foreign country to generate dirt on a potential candidate to diminish the reputation and standing of that candidate - Joe Biden - a perceived front runner in the 2020 national election.

2. To establish an artificial credence for a Russian generated misinformation put forward by Putin to show that it was actually; Ukraine using a server-- CrowdStrike -- in Ukraine -- to hack into the 2016 election helping the Resident get elected - rather than Russin involvement. Well, wasn't that just special?

Apparently, to the Resident, Ukraine was the country that he wanted to gin up evidence to show that Ukraine had done the dirty work in the 2016 election instead of Russia. The server was called CrowdStrike and was purported to be in the Ukraine and used to hack into the Democratic party's emails and publish on WikiLeaks. The problem was; CrowdStrike Is a cybersecurity tech. company based in Sunnyvale, CA. The company has been involved in investigations of several high-tech cyberattacks, including the 2014 Sony Pictures hack, the 2016 Democratic National Committee email leak and the 2015-2016 Democratic National Committee cyber attacks. (CrowdStrike - Wikipedia -- en.m.wikipedia.org)

CAJOLED

Even though there may have been earlier discussions and indications of what the administration had wanted Zelensky of the Ukraine to do it was spelled out in the July 25th call to Volodymyr Zelensky. In that call after V. Zelensky indicated he was very much in need of getting military hardware - Javelin missiles - the answer was 'I would like you to do us a favor though.' 'because our country has been through a lot and Ukraine knows a lot about it. I would like you to find out what happened with this whole situation with Ukraine..' The Resident then indicated what he wanted in terms of an investigation of the Biden's and a look into the CrowdStrike interference into the 2016 election. 'People want to find out about that, so whatever you can do with the Attorney General would be great. It sounds horrible to me.' He should get in touch with William Barr and Rudy Giuliani to try and help with an investigation into the actions of a company involving Hunter Biden. It also involves Joe Biden, a potential Trump rival to the White House in 2020. Though not entirely spelled out here - with the other details that have been gained - that the $400 million had been held up just days before this call - it seems clear that this was a bribe or basically a Quid Pro Quo between the Resident and Zelensky.

CHEATED

Apparently, he was going to use taxpayer money - not even his own - as a bribe to get dirt from Zelensky in the Ukraine to enhance his chances for re-election. How dirty can you get? It is bad enough to bribe another person and use your own money but apparently using our taxpayer money to bribe the head of a foreign government to get dirt on a 2020 candidate in exchange for our taxpayer money - not even his to use - is monstrous! There are a couple other words for this: 1. extortion and 2: Quid Pro Quo, which the Republicans like to use all the time. But the bottom line is: both terms are bribery - as stated as a cause for Impeachment - in the Constitution.

Two Federal crimes seem committed in this one act - mind you. The first is; bribery seems committed which is part of the Constitutionally mandated grounds for Impeachment. And two; 52 U.S. Code Sigma 30121 'Contributions and Donations by Foreign nationals.' 'It shall be unlawful for a person to solicit, accept or receive a contribution or donation of money, or other thing of value, or to make an express or implied promise to make a contribution or donation, in connection with a Federal election.' These crimes seem to break the law!

Under the United States office of the Special Counsel there is a provision for a Whistleblower act to preserve and protect the sanctity and integrity of the Constitution. Below is a:

Whistleblower awareness poster.

Whistleblowing

A "Whistleblower" discloses information he or she reasonably believes evidence:

- A violation of any law or rule
* Gross mismanagement

- A gross waste of funds

* An abuse of authority
* A substantial and specific danger to public health
* A substantial and specific danger to public safety

The office of special counsel (OSC) provides a secure channel through which current and former federal employees and applicants for federal employment may make confidential disclosures. OSC evaluates the disclosures to determine whether there is a substantial likelihood that one of the categories listed above has been disclosed. If such a determination is made, OSC has the authority to require the head of the agency to investigate the matter.

U.S. OFFICE OF SPECIAL COUNSEL
1730 M STREET, N.W., SUITE 218
WASHINGTON, DC 20036-4505

A whistleblower filed a complaint on August 12th about the Resident's conversation with a foreign leader, ultimately setting off a formal impeachment inquiry in the House of Representatives.

The complaint cites "more than half a dozen officials" who gave an account of Trump's call with Ukrainian president Volodymyr Zelensky on July 25th. The whistleblower, who says he was not directly involved with the call, says the person was "deeply concerned" about a potential abuse of the law.

The Inspector General for the intelligence committee wrote a letter to acting Director of National Intelligence Joseph Maguire about the complaint on August 26th. Maguire testified before the House Intelligence committee on Thursday.

*What follows is beginning of the whistleblower complaint:

August 12th, 2019   UNCLASSIFIED

The Honorable Richard Burr
Chairman
Select Committee on Intelligence
United States Senate

The Honorable Adam Schiff
Chairman
Permanent Select Committee on Intelligence
United States House of Representatives

Dear Chairman Burr and Chairman Schiff:

36   I am reporting an "urgent concern" in accordance with the procedures outlined in 50 U.S.C Sigma 3033(k)(5)(A). This letter is UNCLASSIFIED when separated from the attachment.

In the course of my official duties, I have received information from multiple U.S. Government officials that the President of the United States is using the power of his office to solicit interference from a foreign country in the 2020 U.S. election. This interference includes, among other things, pressuring a foreign country to investigate one of the President's main domestic political rivals. The President's personal lawyer, Mr. Rudolph Giuliani, is a central figure in this effort. Attorney General Barr appears to be involved as well.

- Over the past four months, more than half a dozen U.S. officials have informed me of various facts related to this effort. The information provided herein was relayed to me in the course of official interagency business. It is routine for U.S. officials with responsibility for a particular regional or functional portfolio to share such information with one another in order to inform policy making and analysis. ....
- I am also concerned that these actions pose risks to US national security and undermine the U.S. government's efforts to deter and counter foreign interference in the U.S. elections. ....

*The above Whistleblower's report to Attorney General opened a whole can of worms to a thorough investigation. Those investigations affirmed the whistleblower's report and led to further investigations that led directly to the Impeachment. Without this complaint, they would not have been able to launch an investigation that led directly to the Impeachment efforts in the House and Senate where it failed in the Senate.

Even though the media did a horrendous job in finding details and sorting out events and the activities of Rudy Giuliani, it took the House Select Intelligence Committee to do a thorough investigation of this "drug deal" as labeled by John Bolton. It was first investigated in closed sessions and then later in open hearings and found out huge amounts of data and information that eventually led to the impeachment of the Resident.

The breadth and depth of this "drug deal" as described by the Committee, boggling the mind; seems so dastardly, devilishly diabolical and proves to be completely devoid of any moral values, scrutiny, common sense or decency and goes 'Way Beyond The Pale' of what any person - any reasonable, sensible person - particularly any president of the United States - would even consider doing. Particularly, since it seems to break two laws of the United States Government.

On December 3rd, 2019, the House Democrats released a 300-page report with their findings from the impeachment investigation into the Resident's dealings with Ukraine, accusing the Resident of placing "his own personal or political interests above the national interests of the United States" and endangering the national security by soliciting assistance from a foreign government to boost his re-election prospects. The report is based on more than 130 hours of public and private testimony by 17 witnesses before three committees over the past two months. Democrats' case against the Resident centers on a delay in military aid to Ukraine and the Resident's request that the Ukrainian president investigate a political rival and unfounded allegations of Ukrainian interference in the 2016 election, as well as efforts to obstruct the impeachment investigation.

For one who wanted the world to believe that they were totally innocent - they'd gone to an extraordinary amount of trouble to cover up what they'd done, were doing and are continuing to do - even as the impeachment proceedings continued.

Defense attorneys and prosecutors know an interesting fact: If you are innocent, it would be totally illogical if a defendant in court would deliberately hide all evidence and testimony on his behalf. If he were truly innocent, he would want everything to come out - all evidence, every witness, every testimony would be shared to prove his Innocence. Anyone that is on trial - or being impeached - would absolutely demand that every manner of favorable testimony must be presented.

On the other hand, if there is absolutely no one who can or will vouch for your actions positively, you are definitely going to suppress every witness, release of documents, testimony or other corroborating factors to try to avoid the unfortunate exposure of damning and incriminating information that most certainly would condemn you and your actions. In the sinister crime world, this may even go so far as witness tampering or eliminating possible witnesses entirely. These in themselves are very serious crimes and solicit severe penalties.

On Tuesday, October 8, 2019, Mr. Cipollone - the White House Counsel - wrote a letter to Nancy Pelosi and the three committee chairs leading the house impeachment inquiry, that stated in so many terms that the Executive Branch would not cooperate with the Legislative Branch of government, with their investigations. This meant; no documents, no witnesses, no testimonies would be provided for what they intimated was a bogus, illegal effort to Impeach the Resident.

When the sycophant GOP lackeys in the Senate, who held the fate of the Resident in their hands, voted him not guilty of the impeachment charges from the House - they essentially released him from the consequences of that Impeachment accusation. The Resident seemingly Chortled to the world that he had been totally exonerated - was totally innocent, never had any cause for concern and was now emboldened to do seemingly more vile, dastardly things because he knew he might be now 'Crowned the Teflon Resident'.

You see, these GOP lackeys, at one recent time, were decent, law-abiding, Constitution defending, Rule of Law believing citizens of the United States and would never have allowed such dastardly deeds to have been performed by any other president - in particular ones of the Democratic Nature -- who now seems totally emboldened, braggadocious, exonerated and a totally obnoxious bully that's painful to bear.

CAPITULATED

After that last paragraph do you really think that he would even consider doing this? Hell no! Never! This seemingly, grandiosity, super narcissistic person would likely never ever consider capitulating that he may or might have done something wrong, improper or might be breaking any laws.

In general, narcissistic people rarely, if ever, admit they have been wrong, haven't been perfect or done everything right. They are braggadocious, boastful and hyperbolic making any situation seem like they were on top of it - completely - and didn't miss a beat or it was a '"perfect letter". This "perfect letter" term even comes up in the most dire of circumstances of this Covid 19 virus pandemic. Oh, just give us a GD break! The chapter suggests we have to rid ourselves of this cancer!

CHAPTER 11
truoC ooragnaK
Or Kangaroo Court backwards

Well, I'm sure you've all heard of famous Kangaroo Courts, which often could be in small towns, perhaps somewhere south of here. When there is a dastardly crime and there seems to be a need for a quick conviction often a hapless person is found on the street that just might have some characteristics that lend itself to being the defendant. Often the trial is held with jury-rigged data, testimonies, evidence and documents to do this. You might say that that person might be convicted in a Kangaroo Court.

I'm speaking about just the opposite or something totally upside down from that - totally orthogonal. What appears in the Senate impeachment trial is a case where it seems that the evidence, documents, witnesses are totally solid that the crime has been committed and the intent of the crime is well known and understood and the crime clearly meets the criteria for the impeachment Clause of the Constitution.

What happened was that even though all of the evidence and documents seemed Ironclad - showing clear intent to break: not one but two laws of the Constitution, the GOP senators voted to acquit the Resident. One broken law was bribery, extortion or quid pro quo and the other was clearly a violation of the The Federal Election Campaign Act of 1971 - 52 U.S.C. Sigma 30101 - which was enacted February 7th 1972 - which is the primary United States federal law regulating political campaign spending and fundraising. The law originally focused on increased disclosure of contributions for federal political campaigns legislation and was passed by the 92nd Congress and signed into law by President Richard Nixon, a Republican president, in April, 1972.

Foreign Nationals: Campaigns may not solicit or accept contributions from foreign nationals. Federal law prohibits contributions, donations, expenditures and disbursements solicited, directed, received or made directly or indirectly by or from foreign nationals in connection with any election - federal, state or local and that includes the Resident of the United States.

So we seem to have a case where the Resident clearly, without any doubt or equivocation - planned and delivered on a plan to not only ask for but would have accepted a contribution - from Ukraine - in kind to aid in his election against a democrat in the 2020 election. By doing this, it appears he clearly broke a law of the United States. The method that was used - using Federal taxpayer money to extract a bribe or an extortion to gain dirt on an opponent candidate - would be breaking a more fundamental law that is spelled out in the Impeachment Clause of the Constitution.

The Republican sycophants, in a case where all of the facts seemed known and verified, did an inverse Kangaroo Court procedure to exonerate the Resident by voting to acquit him in the Senate Impeachment trial.

Even in light of an overwhelming, compelling body of data and evidence that seemingly showed the intent and execution of the multiple crimes - the defense attorneys appeared to use nearly every obfuscation, twisted, unheard of, arguments of dubious standing to make a case that none of the facts made any difference. It seems that they looked the other way and prodded the GOP to acquit. It would seem to be hard to find a bigger, more flagrant miscarriage of justice.

CHAPTER 12
Those White House Attorneys

During the Impeachment trial in the Senate we were treated to what seemed to be very odd behaviours of the White House Attorneys. Frankly, it was embarrassing just to watch. They seemed to be tying themselves into pretzels trying to make seemingly ridiculous and infantile arguments -explaining why the Resident can't be impeached! Pure garbage. Would it be possible to be disbarred in a regular court for obfuscation, convoluted reasoning and deliberate misinformation? I realize attorneys may be thought of in the worst of terms but they might have to look a long way up, to even get to that stature.

What do they do when they go home and face their wives and children? Do they not have respect for their profession, their honor, respect for themselves and respect for the Rule of Law and morality? What if their children seem more savvy and discerning about the possible damage or the possible destruction of our very institutions - that hold us all together as the greatest democracy? How will they explain to their children their involvement that might have propagated this travesty - when later it might become clear that the shit has hit the fan and we have transmogrified into a russia-nation?

We, England and others went to war to finally save Europe and Africa from that long creeping and finally successful rule of tyranny. Who in Hell is going to come here to save us from our succumbing to the very same fate if it happens? With the possible destruction of the Rule of Law and the foundation of our constitution, where will we go and how will we proceed and on what grounds would we even consider overturning a minority imposed tyranny, possibly leading to a dictatorship?

While I'm on that topic, where will these attorneys be and what might they be saying, or arguing, if all that shit hits the fan? What might they do to try to fix something that they presumably knew they might have played a possible part in a path to destruction? How can they go home at night?

Achim's edge or the 'point of no return' is a law in physics that's well known. Some things in politics or business may flow one direction and reverse and flow back in the other direction. That is ebb and flow. Unfortunately, though, there are situations where if it flows too far in one direction it crosses a line - a point of no return - a situation that cannot be ever reversed - cannot be fixed - cannot be restored.

Such a serious case is that leading to the total destruction of all civilizations and the very world we live on, and the very lives that we lead. That may be called global warming. Just a couple more degrees of warming of the environment of our world and we will cross a line leading to the ultimate irreversible destruction of our lives and civilizations. This will take us all off the Earth forever. Forever is an infinite time!

As bad as that is, the one we are facing right now today in the Senate trial - may be almost as destructive and serious and important as that of the result of global warming. If these attorneys prevail, at the very least, we might just as well start putting voting booths in the Kremlin in Moscow, the Imperial palaces in both Beijing and Puynong or the Imperial palaces in Riyadh, Saudi Arabia or Ankara, Turkey.

As bad as this sounds and it seems, it is by no means anywhere near how bad it could be if this Resident is let off the hook from what appears he may have done in the Ukraine and may be about to be allowed to do it again and again.

44   Far worse for the future, in this Senate trial, that seems dominated by these pretzel bending attorneys the question is: - are they really working for us or the Resident? To be let off the hook by this trial, this Resident would seem to be encouraged to commit more acts of omission regarding our Constitution - some that he may not have even contemplated as yet. I mean, much worse things that he may yet to think of or may be suggested to do by his apparently foreign sources.

It is totally impossible to forgive those who definitely knew better; to consciously, deliberately and actively do what they knew was ultimately going to lead to the destruction of our Democracy - this Republic of these United States - and to the detriment of every living soul that has enjoyed this glorious Freedom of Democracy in these United States for over 240 years. Frankly, I'm not ready for it to end and I know a lot of people who are not ready for it to end. I definitely know that almost the entire United States is not ready for this to end - particularly not in this way! They love Freedom too much!

If we haven't thought about it a lot already, it's time that we start thinking about it a lot right now - particularly now we as a nation - part of the greater world - are facing one of the greatest catastrophes as part of a viral pandemic that has shaken the world, its people and economies, by its Grip.

Those who would willingly, or otherwise, work to destroy our democracy, must be rebuked now and often - in the press, in the news, in media, books, print, plays, drama and in movies - other effective means possible! It must somehow get through to those seemingly blind - almost cultist like followers - that would seemingly follow a pied piper over the proverbial cliff just like in the lemmings myth. It just must be done now!

A WOULD be SUPPORTING ATTORNEY?

It seems there may be an attorney that may just not be deliberately deceptive. If he is a shill, it may seem of the worst kind. To the observer, it appears he tries to be a totally independent, disinterested expert but never as an ally. The modus operandi seems that of a shill working with a snake oil barker. One who is operating as a kind of shill - a totally innocent bystander who just happens by when something totally illogical happens, (totally unbelievable) while a shell game is in operation by a con man doing a shake down.

It seems that whenever the Resident does something really odd, unusual or seemingly against all the rules and laws, he just happens to pop up claiming total independence. The sequence seems to fit this pattern. I don't know him. I didn't vote for him. I'm Independent. I have zero interest in what he does. But you know, I am a distinguished Constitutional expert, and it just happens that what he just did - that you were all whining and crying about - seems to be consistent with the law and the Constitution. You know. You just have to get over your worries about it because I'm the totally disinterested famous attorney that has just proclaimed that he has not broken the law or violated the constitution. Got it?

So here are my thoughts and I offer them for free. He seems to always just show up to defend whatever ridiculous, illogical things, the Resident has just committed. That's the worst kind of shill. Is he really working for the Resident? Is he actually advocating for him and pretends his innocence and Independence in the process? Does he just suddenly show up to seem more valid? Hey, was he one of the W.H. attorneys in the trial who made an awful lot of noise? For one who isn't singing the song, he sure is tapping out a mess of rhythm!

CHAPTER 14
THEY CLAIMED HE did it MORE Than ONCE

An attorney's Rebuttal on Saturday stated that the Resident has actually committed the same crime spelled out in Article 1 of the Impoundment Control Act quite a number of times.

Under this law the Resident has absolutely no Authority to delay or withhold funds that have been allocated by the Congress. Under certain specific cases, if there seems to be an issue of legality, impropriety or corruption, the Resident must go to Congress to appeal the case and only Congress can actually authorize the impoundment or delay of those funds until that condition has been corrected. The Resident may have already broken this law about a half dozen times without doing - what is required by law - to go to congress to obtain approval to change the time or terms of the payment.

This was spelled out by an attorney in his Saturday morning summary as having been done to about a half-dozen other countries including Pakistan and Costa Rica without any congressional approval. Therefore, by his own admission, the Resident may have broken this law a number of times before. Therefore, it has been stated that the law under Article 1 may have been broken at least one time and perhaps five or more times. How many more times has this law been broken?

The Republicans keep arguing that there have been no crimes committed and yet there seem to be many. The first possible crime is simple. If the Resident asked a foreign government to interfere - on his own behalf - in order to cheat in the 2020 election for his own personal advantage, that would violate the FEC voting law of the United States of America that states that "it is absolutely illegal for anyone to solicit, accept or receive anything of value from a foreign National in connection with any election in the United States". Further stated; something of value includes derogatory information that may affect the position of a candidate or campaign in an American election.

It may be asked for, politely or asked for, not politely. He may even demand, cajole or threaten. No matter the style - the act of asking - is the crime! The crime is the asking! There does not have to be a result of any kind to be guilty of committing the crime. There does not have to be a successful result! It does not have to offend the person/country that was asked!

He seemingly asked for that 'favor' in the released transcript of his phone call on July 25th. If so there's no need for further evidence. No need for a Quid Pro Quo. No need for evidence of any other crime. The crime - Bribery - is specifically spelled out in the Constitution as a cause for Impeachment.

Bribery, or extortion, could be from not only asking but then 1. using the status and power of office and 2. leveraging the funds allocated by the people of the United States to extort a personally desired result from another country - that's at war with an adversary of ours, Russia - to hold that as a bribe or an extortion lever to get the investigation that he may want to cheat in the election. If so, that is a crime spelled out by the Constitution even though there were no such laws of the land that had been passed when the Constitution was written. However, the understanding, even then, of what bribery was had been universally understood from British law.

So why is it such a mystery to those in the Senate that this man may have committed bribery, or had the balls to use our taxpayer money to bribe another country for his own personal again to cheat in the 2020 election? If so, talk about adding insult to injury by not even using his own money to bribe or extort in the election. If so, using authority that did not belong to him or using taxpayer's money to cheat to win an election seems to be nothing short of pure Hubris - or Gold Plated Balls. There cannot be any more heinous crime against the United States than that because not only would that be a crime in itself in the common sense but committing a crime against the United States of America and in so doing, aiding and abetting a stated enemy and adversary - Russia.

In this regard is it not possible that this might be considered a charge of treason against the United States by aiding and abetting an enemy of the United States to our disadvantage? The result might be placing the entire United States at a total security risk in its fight against the aggressive advances of Russia. This could be so serious it is totally unacceptable and if left unchecked by this impeachment trial - it may be done over and over again. He could be emboldened to do more unspeakable things that he has not yet even imagined or possibly not yet even conceived by think tanks in Russia.

We cannot! We must not let this happen. To try to vote him out in November while he seems to be blatantly cheating and using Russia and other governments to secretly tilt the playing field to win the election is simply not an acceptable option. The seemingly committed crimes, would help him cheat and perhaps win that election. It seems clear that this may have happened in the 2016 election where Russia purportedly intervened to help select him as the Resident. Hillary's 3,000,000 votes to the advantage over him in the election was not enough to beat him in the electoral college. There seems that there may have been documents hacked and released through WikiLeaks that may have changed the

outcome of the election in the Resident's favor. I don't
know how many times he's bragged about how "I love Wikileaks". The very same Wikileaks that Russia used to distribute the emails that Russia hacked from Hillary Clinton's campaign servers and the DNC servers as well.

On July 27, 2016 the Resident retorted in Florida: "Russia, if you're listening. I hope you're able to find the 30,000 emails that are missing. I think you will probably be rewarded mightily by our press"! Just 5 hours later Russian hackers attacked and acquired numerous damaging emails from Democratic Campaign servers. Wikileaks then distributed them widely at a most crucial time just before the election.

Since being elected he seems to be promoting the Putin playbook. The result of this process appears to be destroying the United States' reputation, its honor, institutions and whatever important other traditions, making us much weaker by the standards or our adversary - Russia. This cannot continue. It must not continue. This cannot happen and cannot go any further. This must stop now! We must all do our part and put aside our differences and unite against this catastrophe that has gripped our great nation before it ceases to be a great nation any longer.

Let me ask just one more seemingly simple question. The answer, to me, seems to be obvious. What kind of person - having considerable authority and responsibility - during the most serious, destructive, dangerous viral pandemic - or plague - the world has seen in a century - when the world is literally fighting for its very survival - would consider using the plague to benefit his friends financially, politically or to either increase or secure his power? Or use it to deliberately anger and set his base against the rest of the Nation? Dumb!!

CHAPTER 15
WE HAVE to THINK like PUTIN

This title encompasses two meanings and texts that support them. The first Is: We need to be thinking like we had always been living in Russia and accustomed and aligned with a life in that oppressive and authoritarian environment. The second is: We need to think like Putin in Russia. We need to know his playbook to understand the events that we are experiencing.

The first is an attempt to understand what is actually going on whenever the Resident seems to take some unexplained action. Such is the case when news people and we do not understand it or don't quite get it. 'Why did he do that?' 'What is going on here?' The reason for our confusion is that we have been living in America for all of our lives and we've lived under the rule of law and under the Constitution. We've lived a way of life that is of those tenets - not like living in Russia.

We tend to trust those in authority and give them the benefit of the doubt. We have always believed that they may have our best interests at heart. We are now dealing with techniques, behaviors, practices, procedures, dramas and goals that are more akin to a life that we might have experienced if we had lived in Russia. That is, living during the Revolution, Post Revolution, then under Stalin and now under Putin. That to us, is a totally foreign way of thinking and a kind of existence that we just do not comprehend; much less can we even imagine it.

We have grown up pretty much trusting the news - at least the reputable news like the New York Times, the Washington Post and the main networks like ABC, CBS, NBC, etc..

There was a time when some newspapers were suspected because they were owned by people who tended to be allied with a political genre and thus slanted. But, we've come to a time for several decades where newspapers and other media, if they're respectable, must of their own accord and by their own direction, verify their sources before presenting the news with confidence. They can't take a risk of just guessing and hoping it will somehow come true after their story airs. It is totally inexcusable and not acceptable in our society to do that. Truth's the root to all freedoms and a vibrant democracy.

We therefore tend to think that politicians, though possibly self-serving, are basically there to do a job that they were sent to do - to represent us and our interests. After all, this is America, a government *by* and *for* the *people*. It is not meant to be a government by and for corporations or the rich. Even though it's getting to be more and more like that, I digress. We tend to take it pretty much for granted. We tend to believe what has been said and we generally don't have to check it out since the newspapers and media make a determined effort to be quite accurate.

So when we hear or see something this Resident does that just doesn't seem to agree with our values, way of life, our beliefs or things that we think America stands for, we just don't understand. Because of our backgrounds, we tend to give the benefit of the doubt. We may assume that we must have mis-understood. Perhaps we just didn't hear it right or correctly. Maybe we didn't get all of the facts. We tend to think; 'why would he do that?' It seems illogical that he's doing something that goes totally counter to common sense.

When he attacks gold star families relentlessly, for example, we think the man has absolutely lost his mind and has no sense of right and wrong. Has he no soul? Was he raised in a closet and fed through the door? No one does that. No one!

52 'Who would do that?' 'Why would anyone do that?' 'What is the point?' 'That is just not done!' It is just not right and yet we've been assaulted by these very same things over and over again on a daily basis. Sometimes assaulted a couple of times a day and as a result they have become all too normalized. Yet, they are still foreign to our ways of thinking and living. And therefore cannot be resolved in our minds or souls. Pundits constantly wonder why he would do anything like that. Who on Earth would do that? Why would any sane man do that? Why would anybody do something so hurtful, harmful and just downright demeaning?

Our lack of understanding is perhaps because we haven't been living in a country like Russia. They lived under the czars, then a Communist regime and now under a 'quote-unquote' democratic government. We don't instinctively understand what goes on in that kind of a world or society where it seems it's dog eat dog and every man out for himself with absolutely no trust of the government or of the politicians.

If we were to begin thinking as if we lived there, I think almost everything we have seen that seems so totally irresponsible, unlikable, unreasonable and unthinking would perhaps be better understood if: that's just the way life is. That's the way it's always been here in Russia and it cannot be changed.

So what is it we need in order to be able to counter what is going on? We all need to understand that form of life. We all need to understand what their kind of thinking is like and what the consequences are. We need to be thinking as Putin thinks and what is in his playbook for America. In fact, I often say, when you hear the news and it's something that just does not seem to make any sense at all: just stop and put in front or behind the sentence; 'in Putin's playbook'. It may not be what we would like to hear but when you put it that way it all seems to make 'sense'.

So much 'sense' it seems abundantly clear: It's to Russia's advantage and to America's disadvantage. It makes Russia more powerful, more significant on the world stage and for America to become a second or third world country by contrast. America would lose its power, lose its influence, lose its Integrity, lose its position in the world economically and politically. It basically becomes a destruction of what we know and what the world has known of the United States for centuries - seemingly a destruction of our way of life, future and our democracy. Putin must be laughing his Arse off.

We have to realize that this has been a dream of Putin and Russia for a very very long time. Particularly, after the demise of Russia as a great nation. As a disgraceful time for Russia it's certainly not one for which to be proud. Putin is trying to change that radically and he's apparently found himself a meme that is very useful for him to tilt the playing field from down toward America to down toward Russia.

If there is a playbook, it likely has been generated in Russia, by think tanks that have looked at our constitution, our laws: the wording of it, the exercising of it and the way it is used. They have studied the laws, the procedures and traditions that have been accepted by almost everybody that runs for an office. What they may have found is that the constitution in general spells out things like rules and laws but seemingly does not prescribe any real means to enforce them. Apparently nothing is spelled out with any enforcement teeth.

54   For example, the emoluments clause. The Resident is not supposed to accept gifts or things of any value from other countries. That is the law. Dirt on an opponent in an election is something of value and the Resident is not allowed to *ask* for or to *receive it. That would be breaking the law.* Using his job to gain huge amounts of wealth from foreign governments is also breaking the law. This might occur when people come here representing foreign governments and rent rooms at his hotels or at his resorts. This might very well be considered as breaking the law of the emoluments clause.

So what is the remedy? There seems to be no remedy spelled out in the Constitution and it appears that there is no legal entity that has standing in the courts to enforce that law.

In the past, whoever was in office, simply respected the law as being what was expected of them. Tradition was being upheld and passed on from generation to generation. They didn't have to be caught, they didn't have to be chastised, they didn't have to be reprimanded, because we lived with the rule of law and that is part of living under the Constitution.

Making this government work is just part of the goal that people who run for governmental offices tend to aspire to. People who basically want to do something good for the government and for the people tend to follow the laws. So they pretty much respect and don't break these laws that are in the Constitution. But when you have a person who believes that he is the law, he just goes ahead and breaks these laws. Who is going to stop you? There's nothing in the laws of the Constitution that can actually be used to stop you from doing it. So why not just let it become normalized and become the normal operation for evermore?

When people tried to go after the use of a hotel as breaking the emoluments clause the court threw the case out because they had no standing in the court. Apparently, no one has any standing because no one can show that they have been aggrieved by the breaking of the emoluments clause. The reason that the constitution does not spell out who is aggrieved by that law being broken is that it is all of us - every citizen. We apparently have no standing in court. Aggrieved?

Well, how in hell are we going to go to court to stop him from doing this? So now that law seems broken forever. These things and things like this, Putin and his think tanks must have figured out a long time ago. Are they passing that knowledge on to the man in the white house in a way for him to be using it to Putin's advantage and benefit? Woo Wee!!

If true, doesn't that just Tork you up something fierce? We are first just totally outraged and then totally frustrated because we realize we have no remedy. Is there no remedy? Is there actually no way to indict him or send him to jail? So the last thing you might do is impeach but that's probably not one of those offenses that would rise to the level of impeachment.

So what is the other half of this dilemma? Putin, and possibly Kim Jung-Un, both strongmen, might be feeding the man in the White House deadly tricks and procedures that could take over this government and make it like a dictatorship. This man seems to admire and fawn over these people who have the strictest kind of power that he seems to think is just absolutely the cats meow. He seemingly wants to be able to act like a strongman and act as if he IS the United States and Congress doesn't matter, the courts, the Supreme Court don't matter, nothing seemingly matters! How very convenient?

56   He apparently thinks he "IS" the United States so if he says something - he speaks for the entire United States.

How do we know that all of this razzle dazzle of going to see Kim Jong-Un about his nuclear war materials actually had anything to do with that subject? I believe their discussions were private. There seemingly were no notes taken. What if he was asking Kim Jong-Un to give him some tips on how to control a nation - absolutely? Can you give me some tips on what things I should do and in what order to absolutely take over a government and people? How do I take a smoothly running democracy and turn it completely into a dictatorship? And now if Kim Jong has done all of this for him, might he not think he's in love with Kim Jong-Un and now he gets very nice love letters from him? Hmmm. Perhaps, very interesting.

Well yes. What do you think he's getting? Do you think he is getting the goods on how to destroy America? Do you think that Putin might be on the same track with all of these sidebar conferences they have at the G7 etc.? I can't imagine they're talking about whether Putin should do this or shouldn't do that. Is it possible that they are talking about how much he's done for Putin and what he might be intending to do when Putin suggests the next step? Like possibly taking over the Department of Justice; the Supreme Court, district courts; the military, the FBI, the CIA or taking over the State Department?

We know he denigrates the press completely making it totally suspect and unreliable in people's minds. Then he denigrates the very members of Congress themselves. Denigrates law enforcement and the chief of law-enforcement, the FBI and the CIA. Denigrates all of them so that no one has a sense of trust and safety under them at all. That's when you have a nation that cannot function anymore because it doesn't trust any of

the institutions that it has loved, lived with and trusted
all of our lives. If we lose trust - we lose all faith in our lives!

This is the rest of the story. If you look at the history of who's taken over countries, they all start with the courts, then the control of news media, control of the justice system and control of the entire Congress - or at least the majority that is needed so there is no hope of getting anything accomplished. This possibly could lead to a process taking place that could very likely destroy all democracy as we know it. Dangerous!

Take a look at ourselves right now. Take a look at America right now. Take a look at the Department of Justice - DOJ. It is seemingly not working for us. It seems to be working for the man in the white house as his own personal fixer. He's stacked the Supreme Court and now through Moscow Mitch has put some 190 high-level justices in courts all over the United States. Constantly, he denigrates the press and particularly those most effective with word - to break through the most secret niches and crannies to discover what dastardly things are happening behind the scenes.

And then he talks about Law and Order - that he is a Law & Order Resident! What Law & Order means to the man in the White House apparently has nothing to do with the Rule of Law. He seemingly has no respect for the Rule of Law but seems to use the law and the courts to exact revenge upon his enemies list or to litigate against those who would oppose him. He seems to believe in courts to do his dirty work to go after people, defend himself, shift the odds of the playing field so that he might win and all of the rest of us just might lose.

He loves the military and loves policemen and police people. Why? Perhaps he seems to think of them as the enforcers of

58   his edicts. Even though he denies it - he seems to be a 'looking the other way kind of guy' tacit supporter of white supremacists and seems to allow them license and cover to do whatever they want even though he denies knowing any of them or having any interest in them at all. However, his actions certainly seem to belie those claims as his actions almost always seem to belie everything else that he claims.

We are so close to the end that it is scary. We seem to have half of the Congress basically doing Putin's dirty work for him. It appears they are taking his misinformation and selling it as being the real skinny. Putin must be laughing his ass off because when he puts something out it seems half of the congress runs with it as if they're spreading cow pie manure.

Congress seemingly is now unwittingly working as Russian agents entirely against America's best interests. Oh God love-em, that just sucks horse puckies! At this point we are at the end of a string that is almost about to break. We've tried impeachment. It was thwarted. Now we have one last shot and that is the election. Damn it. We've got to get it right. We have to get it right and keep it right and destroy this cancer that seems to be eating all of us and would affect all of our lives for a very long time if we fail. 'Never' - has a very ominous ring.

 * * * * By William Shakespeare: from Macbeth.   Tomorrow, and tomorrow, and tomorrow, Creeps in this petty pace from day to day, To the last syllable of recorded time; And all our yesterdays have lighted fools The way to dusty death. Out, out, brief candle! Life's but a walking shadow, a poor player, that struts and frets his hour upon the stage, And then is heard no more. It is a tale Told by an idiot, full of sound and fury, Signifying nothing. ...

How often that we must reflect upon these sentiments lest we be heard from no more!! Our duty as citizens is very clear!!

WHERE ARE the 12 DECENT PEOPLE?

I can't tell you how many times during the past 3 years I've just cried out after a long newsday: 'where in hell are 12 decent, law-abiding, upstanding, people who might march into the Oval Office, wrap the Resident in a straitjacket, shove him into a closet and put a cardboard cutout of him behind the desk? So many times, it seems - sometimes on a daily basis - for the things being done in this country - seemingly not for it, that seem so awful, so terrible, so demeaning and downgrading to the dignity of these United States - that somewhere, somehow, there has got to be at least twelve, reasonable, honorable, clear thinking, decent, capable people that know what's best and must take action to mitigate it.

For example, who in the hell in their right minds would let the Resident have a meeting with Putin by himself with not even note takers, or if there are notes, allow them to be destroyed? The very same thing goes for those meetings with Kim Jong-Un. What kind of Insanity would it take to even think that a meeting would be in the best interests of the United States government, particularly if there are suspicions there may be close functional ties between Putin and the Resident that may have led to his selection in 2016? Even if these were only suspicions, no board of directors of a company would ever allow such an abortive meeting to occur. Where is the board of directors of the United States who could step in and say to the Resident: 'I'm sorry, that is not allowed by our Charter, our Mission Statement or our operating principles.'

When he goes to see Kim Jung-un, presumably to talk about the Denuclearization of North Korea - because the meeting is private - might he in fact be talking about how to take over the freedoms of a democracy? A democracy such as the

60   United States? What steps to take first? What steps to take next? What steps to secure the results in an irreversible way that cannot be overturned except by a foreign army as the free world did in the 2nd world war?

We are seemingly like the people of Europe during World War II who knew all too well what had happened to their life and their freedoms. They knew all too well the results of this kind of takeover but were totally helpless to do anything about it, to stop it, to change it or to alter it in any way. It had gone past the Rubicon -   the point of no return   - forever. We are seemingly at that point now with only one last hope remaining. The hope of the 2020 election - which we know all too well - that Putin may have his thumb on the scales and might do his best to tilt the playing field so that no matter how many of us vote - the Resident may still be likely to be re-elected.

If that happens, we might as well all become refugees and try to find some other place to go and live - perhaps Australia, New Zealand, Canada or Mexico. Any other place but here. The results would be too devastating, too complete, too horrifying to contemplate. We are already there in some aspects. So much so that I say: people, open your eyes and see what's already happened in just the last month and know that this has to be stopped, to be reversed. This cancer must be eliminated now. Hey, you GOP rallying tribes? You may be detrimentally affected even more than everyone else by the results. Your lives likely will be ruined even more than the rest of us. Thank you so GODDAMN MUCH for your just looking the other way!

While I'm on the subject, where are those 12 reasonable men in Congress or governors who everyone knew at other times to be clear thinking, rational public servants that would've known what to do rather than be sycophant lackeys? DAMN it!

WORLD WIDE PANDEMIC

I just had to throw this short chapter in because it seems so pertinent to what was actually happening at the moment and sheds a lot of light on the capability, the intent or the possibly destructive thinking of this Resident. Putin's Plan? Hmmm.

The Covid-19 virus started in Wuhan China sometime early December and the United States became aware on the 22nd of January. The Resident, as anybody would, restricted travel from China to the United States shortly after learning of the virus. There were cruise ships and people on Airlines that were coming into the United States and they were held up to quarantine on the ships or removed to quarantine here in the United States. All very necessary moves to try to minimize the spread of this virus into the United States. Bravo for him!

As the virus was gaining strong footholds in Washington and southern California, the Resident seemed to want it to appear that we had done everything needed and these numbers might increase a bit but it would die back down and just go away. Poof! It seemed evident that he didn't want to have large case numbers indicating a worldwide pandemic on his watch - especially in an election year. Several times it was claimed to be just Democrats fake news - that it could be just a hoax drummed up to make him look bad during the upcoming election. 'Dems wanted it to last to look bad'.

Well, then there was this: All of the medical experts who know about new viruses - ones that have no immunity in the society - know that the number of cases will double in a matter of two or three days and that's going to be a worldwide plague. I mean, that it will produce - in just a month or two - devastating worldwide events - exhibiting hundreds of thousands of cases.

62   Ok, it goes; 64, 128, 256, 512, 1024, 2048, 4096 so that in just 19, 3 day steps, that number is 524,288 cases in only 57 days. It's an exponential curve that was known before 1/22/20. Now let me see - from January 22 that could be March 19th. That's just a few days ago. The worldwide number is now 462,555. (The rate was off a bit.) The deaths are now at 20,876 or 4.5% of worldwide cases. It could've been known - 1/22/20!

Actually, it doesn't take a rocket scientist to know that. A childhood student using basic math would have known that quite readily. But even ignoring that, epidemiologists around the world - and that were in the White House until removed in 2018 - as apparently being unnecessary - would have had that knowledge readily available to predict how serious this was.

There are now 54,453 cases and 737 deaths at 1.4% in the U.S. If only 20% of those require acute medical attention using respirators and other PPE (Personal Protective Equipment) that would be 10,891 acute cases possibly in the United States by March 25th. We are fortunate that our death rate seems lower than the worldwide percentage right now.

Keep in mind that these numbers can double in just about 3 days. That could be 21,782 acute cases and 1,474 deaths in the U.S. by the end of the month. That could be 105,256 acute cases and 23,584 deaths by - Easter Sunday! No wonder Gov. Cuomo is panicking. This is nothing to take lightly or to try to "edict/declare" away or mitigate by political - wishful thinking.
  • Actual Easter # was 525,000 cases and 21,500 deaths **
It's just not possible for anyone - by strength of will, sheer determination or even an executive order - to cause it not to happen. Trust me, it takes a lot more than an executive order. Planning had to have started two months or more ago to start ordering someone to make ventilators. This is something you

don't set up in two days or one or two weeks. It probably
takes several months or more to set up and deliver them.

This requires acquisition of materials - that requires a supply chain established. Parts have to be produced, assembled and tested. This is no simple matter. It's not like making gloves or facial masks. It is a horrendous job and you can't just say, 'well, we have plans for those who think they can do it if only they'll step up to it'. No, it could be six months. Look at those numbers that could be there by Easter if this isn't mitigated.

This is no time for wishful thinking and happy talk! Realities should have set in two months ago and deliberate Residential action taken when they learned of this pending pandemic in January. It appears they buried their heads in the sand and hoped it would just go away. 'It's a hoax'. 'It's a democratic campaign ploy' the Dems set to defeat the Resident in 2020.'

Decisive action should have been taken to avert the situation before now. It is just not acceptable to do nothing - or in this case - possibly very little. It is clearly way too late to have taken decisive action to avoid the numbers that I've shown above. Thank God there are responsible governors that have taken bold measures to try to mitigate this disaster but desperately needed help from the Federal government; FEMA, the Army Corps of Engineers, Defence Production Act and a national plan for mitigation of this type of well understood viral pandemic. I'm one of those being displaced by this viral pandemic and I'm not sympathetic at all with anyone - I mean anybody - that should've known what to do to bend the curve down quickly to minimize the horrible personal and financial effects that we are all facing. It affects all our lives! If a person drags his feet from initial confusion - he generally changes - but if not - <u>it may be for another reason or another person</u>!

CHAPTER 18
DEMOCRACY DIES - WHEN BASED on LIES!
When TRUTH DIES >>> the FATE of DEMOCRACY LIES

Could the Coronavirus be more effective than a Neutron Bomb?

1. A truth can form only a single line between points A and B.
2. There's only one line, of many, that's true between A and B.

In other words, if there are two or more lines between A and B only one can be true.   So, if there are many lines between A and B - ALL OF THEM are LIES except possibly one, because only one of them can be the truth! Should be so very obvious.

Lies, however, can form thousands of lines between A and B. If many lies are generated between A and B, perhaps tens or thousands of them, it is a moot point because it is almost impossible to find one truth out of hundreds. Therefore, If you never tell the truth and everything is a different lie, then you are generating myriads of lies - that all just might appear to many people as being the truth. But, by an overwhelming history, perceptive ones know; *all must be considered as lies*.

This allows you to pick the best one later to answer a question. You can point to THE one lie that agrees with the challenge and therefore ignore the hundreds of others that don't. Guess what? By this M.O., you can always have the right answer for the situation at hand. By this process you cloud the issues and are obfuscating the truth in a way that it's almost impossible for anyone to distinguish what is true anymore. Almost impossible from now on! Remember all lies!

So, if we are drowning in a sea of Lies and reaching for the single truth, ie. the Lifesaver to save us - it is impossible to find it in that sea of Lies. Lies and Truth, by then, all look alike and seemingly everyone could be the truth. But they're not!

So if the White House says something about alternate facts - and everyone knows that there are no alternate facts - it's likely intended to obfuscate away from the actual truth.

This is simple enough to understand but what does this really mean? I suppose it means at the very least that you can be everything to everyone and can easily satisfy everyone's needs of the moment - to their satisfaction. Everyone hears exactly what they want to hear and nothing contradictory. However, as bad as that sounds, it turns out to be far more sinister than that. It Is, orders of magnitude, far more sinister - branching out - possibly to be even more totally destructive.

When a democracy is swimming in a sea of lies and cannot find the truth, it is going to drown in that sea, leading to a total disaster. Democracy and the rule of law depend upon knowing the facts or the truth to make the right decisions or convictions. Lawmakers cannot construct or pass laws if they don't have a true basis upon which to build them. They must have the truth - the facts - on which to make the right decisions. It is impossible to fashion laws or enact legislation if none of the basis has any truth in fact. All are considered as lies and so the source must always be *considered irrelevant*!

If it's based upon lies, democracy dies! A democracy cannot exist in a sea of Lies where it has no basis, no facts and no foundation whatsoever to build upon. If you are in the sea of lies, what difference does it make if you add just a few more drops of water (propaganda)? Drip, drip as our democracy washes away in a total tsunami of lies. Democracy ceases to exist. Just kiss it all goodbye! *Covid 19 virus note: Page 69.

Just think back on the past three years and what is it that you really recall the most? One thing that stands out in those three years is that the Resident in the white house has told more than 16,000 lies in roughly a thousand days. That could be 16 Lies per day or several per sentence. Have any of those lies helped any of you understand what is going on? Have any of those lies helped explain how he was selected rather than the one who won 3 million more popular votes? Have any of those lies confirmed what this person promised he would do to help you, the American People? Have any of these lies helped exonerate this person or defend his behavior in the Ukraine, Russia or North Korea?

Many more pages with similar questions and you'd still not run out of examples of what this person has seemingly not done for you through lying! Think back. I think you could fill five more pages of such questions by yourselves. Fact number 1: it's generally believed he rarely tells the truth. The president of the United States - the leader of the Free World -The Beacon of democracy **MUST NOT TELL LIES**. The very nature of this post - its position, its prestige, its insights, just cannot be filled by a person that tells lies! It does not work for America or for the world. It should be the absolute minimum requirement to be allowed to occupy that high position.

How many wrongs make a right? How many lies make a truth? One? ten? How many lies does it take to make our one truth? 1,000, 10,000? It turns out, it took 16,000 lies to make our one truth: that this man seems unfit to be Resident of the United States. Always telling the truth, should be the first absolute minimum requirement for the job of president of the United States. Always being truthful is the first requirement of any job application that I've filled out whether I've been successful or not. Why was it not the absolute first requirement to be qualified to be president of these United States - the most powerful position in the world? Was it just

overlooked? Did we miss it somehow? Was the box just
not checked? Explain to me how this could have happened!

How many lies does it take to *Fake* America great again? How many lies does it take for Mexico to pay for the wall? How many lies does it take to bring jobs back? How many lies does it take to try to show that jobs came back to the United States when it seems the net-net is nearly zero? How many lies does it take to Drain the swamp? How many lies does it take to get the farmers soybean markets back into China? How many lies does it take to get North Korea to denuclearize its military? How many lies does it take to save the souls of those poor children and families at our Southern border?

How many lies does it take to keep the world from knowing how much Russia did in the '16 election? How many lies were told about talks with high-level Russian contacts during the campaign? How many lies does it take to cover up those vital connections - Russia - seemingly in the campaign? How many lies were to cover those possible connections with high-level Russians during the campaign? How many lies does it take to claim that Russia had nothing to do with the 2016 campaign? How many lies does it take to claim his inauguration had the largest crowd ever - particularly bigger than Obama's? How many lies does it take that Putin knew better than our own secret service and Intelligence and Security Agencies?

How many lies does it take to claim that the denuclearization treaty with Iran was terrible and needed to be abandoned? How many lies does it take to claim that the Paris global warming accords needed to be abandoned? How many lies does it take to claim that there is no such thing as global warming, whether man-made or not? How many lies does it

68   take to claim that Saudi Arabia had nothing to do with the brutal assassination of Khashoggi? How many lies does it take to claim that NAFTA was a terrible agreement and then replace it with NAFTA2 - essentially the same as NAFTA but with some benefits the Democrats added before it passed?

How many lies does it take for an attorney to claim that the Resident has absolute inalienable rights Under Article II that - whatever he believes is justified - cannot be challenged? How many lies does it take to cover up a Ukraine Bribery and Extortion scheme? How many lies does it take to try to promote the Putin misinformation that Ukrains interfered in the '16 election instead of Russia? When do we stop hearing possible lies about the independence of the DOJ from the Resident of the United States?

I could go on with this list but you know them better than I do. You know them all! You've seen them - you've heard them - you've lived them. Where does it stop? When do we finally take this to heart and eliminate a cancer that has slowly grown into the very soul of America and is devouring our Democracy? How many more lies will it take? Another thousand, ten thousand? Perhaps sixteen thousand or more?

None of our lives have that much time left to survive this. None of this nation has more than a few months to survive this cancer if allowed to continue to grow for even one more year. There will be nothing to live for and no place to live in or grow our careers or families. Every soul and existence of this great Democracy - the beacon of hope - the most powerful nation in the world might become shriveled to a third world dictatorship. And no one in this world will come to save us like we did Europe during the Second World War. Heaven Help Us, for we must have strength beyond our own souls and our own grit to rid this great nation of this terrible, terrible cancer that seems to be eating at the very Heart of America.

Folks here's the deal. We're no longer approaching the brink! We have already crossed the red line, the Rubicon. We have gone beyond the point of possibly no return by breaking, destroying and abandoning the rule of law - the very heart, soul and basis of this Democracy. When we totally ignore the tenets of the Constitution and the tenets of the rule of laws and principles; we no longer have this beloved democracy that we have loved and shared for over 240 years. It just could cease to exist. FOREVER!

* Covid 19 pandemic note.

While editing and proofreading written chapters, the United States has changed dramatically in as little as one month - just 30 days - that's all. A Covid 19 virus initiated in Wuhan China in November, 2019 - spread to the United States and was known in the United States as early as January 2020. China travel was stopped almost immediately and cruise ships were quarantined in place and airplanes downloaded to quarantine here in the United States. This measure was so obvious that anyone would have taken it. However, the virus quickly took hold in California and Washington state. For a month-and-a-half the Resident seemed to tweet hyperboles to try to minimize the image of the virus - as it proceeded to New York and expanded exponentially as a worldwide pandemic. Feb. 10th: 'looks like by April, you know, in theory, when it gets a little warmer, this miraculously just goes away.' Feb. 28th: 'This is the Democrats new hoax.' March 4th: 'based on a lot of conversations with a lot of people that do this, because a lot of people will have this and it is very mild. They will get better very rapidly...' The lies seemingly flowed faster than --> action, that was seemingly abandoned when critically needed!

70   While giving press conferences on a daily basis to blare to his enamored base about the tremendous wonderful things he was doing to try to stop deaths in the United States, in fact it seemed very little to nothing was being done during two extremely crucial, life saving, pandemic controllable - months.

Tens of thousands of respirators were going to be needed by mid-April because an exponential curve shows that's just where the virus was going to be in the tens of thousands of patients. Manufacturers had to be conscripted immediately by the end of January by the Defense Production Act to start building respirators that would be needed in the tens of thousands by mid April to stem the Covid 19's exponential expansion. Lies seemed to flow faster than PPE components that were desperately needed by the millions - on a daily basis - in hospitals all over the United States. Especially in NY state.

By this date, the Defense Production Act has not been applied to start building needed respirators. Promises and pronouncements of what a wonderful job the Resident has been doing seems to be the largest production to date. The self-aggrandizing pronouncements seem to be aimed at the base to shore up what could be a disastrous situation in the coming election. It seems it's more important to have a good image - even if many lives might die - than to tell the truth and do something to solve this life-threatening pandemic in the United States - albeit, the entire world. What a terrible cost!

This is the very worst possible case to show why Lies may kill Lives. No matter the intent or motivation - the effect is the same. The truth might have saved tens of thousands of lives - taking responsibility is all that it requires. If feet dragging, at first, isn't replaced - who may know? It may have, yet, quite a different basis. WHEN WE LIVE ON LIES - AMERICA DIES!

Corona Virus or COVID 19

I wasn't going to write it. I wasn't going to do it. I thought I could get by without it but this has become so very important that it just could not be ignored. This gets to the very heart of why this book was written. It goes to the very foundation of everything and every reason - that this book is being written.

There have been so many times - so very many times - that it seemed like when the Devil was about to get its Due - every time - it slipped away like an ant through a crack or like water through a sieve. Gone. So disappointingly - everytime.

Well, maybe in real estate one can use hubris and hyperbole to bluff his way through a bad deal. Perhaps in politics one can continue to put a positive face on something which is going terribly, terribly wrong. Perhaps in a Reality TV show one can make anything look better than it actually is and create truths, realities, alternate facts and somehow make them all seem just so real and, more importantly, believable.

How many times have we seen this? How many times have we thought this was finally it? It was finally going to come crashing down. How many times have we seen it just slip away - as if by the very breath of the devil - by some further feat of hubris, hyperbole, lies and deceits? Well, way too many! It's like a Teflon Resident. But, do you know that a virus - Coronavirus, this particular virus - doesn't watch television, it doesn't read newspapers, it doesn't do Twitter or read Twitter accounts, it doesn't hear the hyperbole, any of the nonsense or happy talk. It just goes on its very deliberate 4, 8, 16, to a hundred thousand, two hundred thousand, four hundred thousand - on its way up to the millions. It just doesn't care! It doesn't read exponential graphs - it just simply makes them!

72   So the Resident says we are going to reopen this country by Easter - just 3 weeks away. He says that he has done the best job ever - a most remarkable job. We have done the best job ever - never done before - never ever in history has this been done. He says that nobody's ever known about this before - could not even imagine something like this could happen. He is the only one who is capable of doing it and is doing it and saving us all right now and has been from the start! (Excuse me while I go off in a corner - and just Vomit!) You too? Hope it went better than mine. Ah, but I digress!

Have we no eyes? Did we not go to school and learn simple basic exponential math curves that start out very small and within a very short time explode to millions in the numbers? A virus doesn't read these grade school math curves - - it MAKES them! It does it on a very simple principle. Have you ever heard of the atomic bomb?

One sick person infects two - those two infect two more. Those four each infect two more making it 8 - and so it goes. An atomic bomb works on the same principle, but it does it so rapidly - in milliseconds - that it literally explodes extremely violently by this chain reaction. This is exactly the same thing of one making two - two making four and four making 8 until the energy can't be contained and it blows up Hiroshima or Nagasaki, ending in a very dramatic tragedy and catastrophe.

The virus does the bomb BIT much slower - literally taking many months to get to huge numbers - but to huge numbers it will get if unchecked or not mitigated by some mechanism to reduce the numbers that each sick person can infect. This is like absorbing moderators used in an atomic pile to slow the chain reaction so it can be used to generate electricity.

The facts are clear. This phenomena has been understood for diseases for at least a century - at the very least the 1918 Spanish flu pandemic and the Swine flu in 2009. Do you remember that one - just 10 years ago? Didn't the Resident hear about what to do about a possible viral pandemic if it came during his time in office? Was not a Pandemic task force set up and running in the White House in 2016 in anticipation of and in order to be prepared for just this event? What happened to that? Why weren't we relying upon that in January of 2020 and taking immediate action to start building 50,000+ ventilators at a time that they might be ready for the very predictable viral pandemic curve in 2 - 3 months that certainly would have been warranted near that time?

In general, a huge crisis is not a time to criticize one who is presumably in charge but herein lies Many Lives. Thousands of lives, maybe tens of thousands of lives, are in the balance of what was, would have or might have been done. Is that not a time to evaluate how well the job is being done when there might still be time to dramatically change the course for the far greater good in saving LIVES? I mean life is at stake here - lives are at stake here - the very thing the Conservative GOP have been screaming about - when it comes to abortion - and every other thing that seemingly is not important now? LIFE!

All of this evaluation should have been done much more effectively, more thoroughly, much sooner, in order to change the course months ago - to save tens of thousands of lives. There is no better time than now to change the course dramatically - albeit a bit too late to save perhaps hundreds or thousands of lives. We all know if this was a large corporation and its product was killing tens of thousands of people - the board would have stepped in months ago and taken the Principal out onto the street if not headed for jail. It's criminal.

CHAPTER 20
WHAT ABOUT THE RULE of LAW?

This is a tough one and it requires a lot of analysis but I will try to make it very short and perhaps not so sweet.

There seems to be no way to sugar coat this, so I just have to say it. The Resident, having been the chief executive of a corporation/LLC - whatever - seems to act as if he worked in an entity that had no board of directors. I could be wrong about that. Apparently, his experience as the boss is that nobody is above him who can say; 'I'm sorry, but you can't do that.' 'That is not what is done.' 'That's not in the best interest of this organization or you could go to jail' - as perhaps it may be against the law or for some other understandable reason.

No matter the reason or the circumstance, that is the way he seems to believe that he can work as the Resident of these United States. Well, it just does not work that way in the United States - or at least it used to not work that way. The government is broken up into three equal parts that provide checks and balances on each other and over the entire system. All of them - without exception - all of them work for us, the people of the United States - their Employer. They all take an oath of office to protect and defend the Constitution and its tenets including the rule of law, which is the very basis of democracy. To do otherwise is to destroy the very foundation and existence of this great nation.

What seems to be observed is that he doesn't believe in the rule of law as it may apply to him. Perhaps he thinks he 'IS' the law to the extent that whatever he says - actually becomes law. No need for legislative or judicial branches. There's an ugly name for just this thing. You all know it - now say it to yourself outloud and hear how bad it sounds in your ears. Just say it!

Apparently he doesn't believe in the rule of law for himself but that doesn't mean that he doesn't believe in the use of law to be used against others. The courts seem to be ineffective against his behavior, but he apparently loves using the courts to go after others in legal actions to impose upon others.

There's an interesting dichotomy - Law and Courts for others but of no value against him. Apparently he just thinks he can ignore them as being irrelevant when it comes to himself. He loves to use the courts to keep people from getting things from him - all the way to the Supreme Court if necessary - but when the courts rule against him it's tended to be ignored. I mean, what are they going to do about it? Who's going to make him obey the court order? Does that sound familiar again? I mean does that not sound like that ugly word that we were saying out loud before? Probably! Yes! But I Hope Not!

Apparently, as long as there's no board of directors that can say, 'I'm sorry, in the federal government we don't do that and you can't do that.' That board of directors normally would be a large group of people with enough clout to walk in and say 'No, this just isn't going to happen'. 'No that's not the way it is.' That group, right now, seems to be the bulk of the GOP party that's in the government. People that normally were rule of law - constitutional law defending and abiding people that, for whatever reason, may be looking the other way. Perhaps they feel that's alright - he's our guy - he can do no wrong.

All we can say is, if that's the deal and there seems plenty of feedback to indicate that's what is believed by his base, then this nation seems to be in a great deal of hurt and trouble and may have really hard times in the future. Perhaps worse than this horrible pandemic and likely suffer much worse, serious consequences for a much longer time. God help us all!

76   The rule of law seems to be now under more severe attack since shortly after the Mueller report. This attack seems to be coming primarily from the one part of the government that is charged to defend the rule of law and to defend the people of these United States against internal and external threats. Instead, the DOJ seems more interested in trying to eliminate the existence of the Mueller report and any or all charges against people that may have been charged as a result of the Mueller investigation.

Let's see if I can put this in perspective. A person who is not part of the government in any way calls a foreign diplomat of a country that has just been sanctioned by the United States government for election meddling. In essence he imports them to not reprimand in kind but to wait until the new government is installed when things might be 'taken care of'. That violates a federal law - the Logan act - enacted January 30, 1799. It criminalizes negotiation by unauthorized American citizens with foreign governments having a dispute with the United States. The intent behind the act is to prevent unauthorized negotiations from undermining the present government's position. Since this law was violated over an issue affecting the outcome of our most sacred institution - voting for the highest office in the land - it represents the greatest security and sovereignty threat that is possible to the United States!

Clearly this is of the highest security interest that can be - the very basis of our democracy - involving both the rule of law and the complete integrity of our ability to elect officials and governments completely without any foreign interference. After pleading guilty twice the defendent changes his plea to not guilty and the DOJ decides to drop the charges as being of no consequence to National security. Now, just how many criminals will suddenly want to do this just to get out of jail?

ELITISM, LAISSEZ-FAIRE and VIGILANTISM,

Elitism: the advocacy or existence of an elite as a dominating element in a system or society. The attitude or behavior of a person or group who regard themselves as belonging to an elite. Further is the belief or attitude that individuals who form an elite -- a select group of people with an intrinsic quality, high intellect, wealth, special skills or experience, -- are more likely to be constructive to society as a whole, and therefore deserve influence or authority greater than that of the others. The term elitism may be used to describe a situation in which power is concentrated in the hands of a limited number of people. Elite theory opposes:

Pluralism: (more than one system of power), a tradition that assumes that all individuals, or at least the multitude of social groups, have equal power and balance each other out in contributing to democratic political outcomes representing the emergent, aggregate will of society.

Laissez-faire: A policy or attitude of letting things take their own course without interfering. Abstention by governments from interfering in the workings of the free market. It means let people do what they choose. It describes a system or point of view that opposes regulation or interference by the government in economic affairs beyond the minimum necessary to allow the free enterprise system to operate according to its own laws.

Vigilantism: is law enforcement undertaken without legal authority by a self-appointed group of people. A vigilante justice, as defined by The Legal Information Institute, is the actions of a single person or group of people who claim to enforce the law but lack the legal authority to do so.

78   Vigilantism itself is not illegal under US law but involves actions that are oftentimes Illegal.

Wondering why these definitions at the start of this chapter? It's an interesting thing but it reflects on confusing aspects of what we've experienced in the last 3 years. They're somewhat orthogonal to each other - yet somehow have been combined in a strange mix of conflicting intents and practices.

You see, elitism is seemingly what the head of this government thinks of itself for the past 3 years. It thinks it's smarter, better, more knowledgeable and more capable than anybody ever could be - ever, ever! And yet, to most thinking people - they have realized that it's not that at all but just might be quite the opposite. Nonetheless, that is a behavior that seems to have been imposed upon the United States.

So now laissez-faire. Where we are taking off every regulation possible on business, environment and all of the things that have been established to try to make our life safe and livable - such as clean air, water, our environment, food and drugs. This includes letting business do whatever it wants to take as much money as it wants and therefore become big business and big money's best friend.

We see vigilantism begin to creep more into our Petty Pace day-by-day - when people with differences of opinion that feel a need to discuss them in a way that could lead to the greater good - are finding themselves on enemy lists - on Blacklists that seem to be targets for governmental investigations and various other means for retaliation. We call a COVID 19 the Chinese Virus and suddenly a large number of natural, long time Chinese and Asian citizens are attacked and harassed. Again the names for this kind of government are very ugly.

MIGHT as well set up VOTING BOOTHS in MOSCOW

Boy, we have really done it haven't we? We have crossed the Rubicon. This impeachment inquiry really opened up a huge can of worms that was crawling beneath the surface - out of sight, until the Whistleblower brought them to the surface to be seen. What forms these worms have taken has expanded our imagination into almost anything if not everything that can possibly go wrong if a Resident might have been selected by a foreign country - bent on destroying the United States.

It seems much of what was found during the impeachment investigation regarding possible bribery and extortion of Ukraine, using taxpayer money and the high position of the presidency, may have been specific to a type of extortion in order to aid and abet the Resident's chances in the 2020 election. However, to those of us who have suspected this from the beginning, it seemed to validate the notion that this is not a unique single first-of-its-kind incident. What has been shown is that this may have been an ongoing activity that might have gone on during the 2016 campaign as well.

Even though we knew Russia was highly involved in the voting manipulation of the 2016 election in favor of the Resident, we have had some doubt as to whether there was a cross connection between his campaign and Russia. The Ukraine investigation seems to dispel any doubt that this has possibly been going on during the '16 campaign and perhaps as far back as the 2013 Miss Universe pageant in Moscow.

The Ukraine investigation seems to reveal a very ugly image of what we might've imagined before - it may be only the tip of the iceberg. This possible involvement against the United States may have been going on at a much deeper, broader

80   level than anybody could possibly have imagined before. It seems improbable he was elected based on what he did himself. This then begs the question. If this is what he did to help get himself selected by using international interference and cooperation, we might just drop the middleman and set up voting booths in Moscow, Beijing, Riyadh and Pyongyang.

Hey, despite that it seems totally unreasonable, the facts seem to show we are pretty much matched nearly 50/50 - Democrat vs Republican - when it comes to elections. From the Democrats standpoint it seems like it should be 90 Democrats 10 Republicans but for whatever strange reasons it doesn't turn out that way. Okay, if that's the case, why do we even bother setting up voting booths here in the United States since that notion will pretty much cancel itself out.

As a result, the election would be determined, as it might have been in 2016, by interference from a place like Russia. If that's the case and we're going to have it normalised, we might as well get used to it. We might as well just set up voting booths in Moscow, Beijing, Riyadh and Pongyang and let them determine the outcome of our election for us - pretty much as they seemingly may have done in 2016.

Think how much easier that would be for people in the U.S. They don't have to worry about getting to the voting booths on days that they work. They don't have to get themselves registered. They don't have to make the effort and stand in those long lines. Think of the cost reduction if we don't have to have precinct voting committees in each state and we don't have to pay for voting machines or places to poll. Just have it all done from outside the country the way it has seemingly been done in the last major election of 2016. Hey, if the result is essentially going to come out the way, Russia, or Beijing

wants it to come out, then let them have at it. We just
become shadows of ourselves and, as the old saying goes, wash our hands of it and accept whatever the results may be.

I mean, what's the difference if we have crooked judges at the Super Bowl and we BET our retirements, homes, jobs, futures on the outcome of the Super Bowl? Hey, whatever happens when the crooked judges make their decision - that's what we have and that's what we will live by. How bad can that be?

Doesn't that just sound great to a casual, laid-back, perhaps lazy electorate? It sure saves a lot of stress on the brain listening to candidates bragging about their capabilities and listening to the harangue between them or the dastardly ads that they run against each other. What could be more simple, what could be more easy, what could be more sane? Laissez-faire and C'est la Vie. Nobody gets upset. Cousins and uncles; fathers and daughters don't get into huge knock-down drag-out fights at Thanksgiving or Christmas. We just all agree to get along and let it all roll out like in Russia?.

Tongue-in-cheek? Yes, tongue-in-cheek. Where in hell are those Republicans who used to believe in the Constitution, swear by the rule of law and the tenets of the Constitution and who hated Russians and called them 'Pinko Commie Lovers'? Where in hell are they when the country seems to be going to hell in a Putinbasket? What do they think they are going to get from this 'person', that it's worth scrapping everything to follow the Pied Piper? Where is the Lemming - Aid? Even though lemmings don't commit suicide jumping off the cliff as in the Myth we might as well believe that they do. So these people, who are following this 'person', are basically running off the cliff - and don't seem to stop to see, care or even consider that the cliff is coming just ahead.

82   They don't even think in terms of a cliff but instead they may think they're doing something spectacular, going up a hill and going to have wonderful times. Well, when it all hits the fan they are going to be part of what hits the fan. And you know how the saying goes; what hits the fan, the fan makes into mincemeat. Enough said! Poor Pinko Commie Lovers!

*Just a footnote: about Amoral vs. Immoral. These Concepts - throughout the writing of this book - seemed to keep popping into my head as to what really is the meaning and what is the difference as if there was such a deep down significance for this book? I was seemingly compelled to find out. Perhaps the reader can extract some significance to the connection.

Both have to deal with right and wrong and therefore if you don't have the definition they might be confusing.

- Amoral; means having no sense of either right or wrong. Doing something and just not knowing better.

- Immoral; describes someone who does know the difference, doesn't care and does whatever he wants - possibly for his own benefit without concern for others.

Oh why oh why, for the life of me, why is it these things kept popping into my head throughout the writing of this book? Do you, as a reader, get the significance? Can you tell me why it is that these things are apparently significant in my mind as I was going through the process of the writing of this book? I bet that you can - without hesitation or contemplation.

THESE DEFENDERS of the CONSTITUTION
The Dark Force vs The Deep, Dark State

By the end of yesterday, 1/31/20, the Senate was so goddamn awful that, perhaps those Senators - might see themselves in a video or just wake up and feel just how mean-spirited they were. Many, if not most, at one time, were normal, living, thinking, reasoning people who might wake up completely horrified, and admit 'how cruel, debased, and mean-spirited we all seemed'. 'That is not who we were!' 'That is not who we are!' 'That is not what America is about!' 'That's not how Americans got to where they were until two or three years ago.' 'It is not how America must be now and in the future!'

So how did it come to this? The gate opened by the apparent disrespect for the Rule of Law, followed shortly thereafter by a road that could lead to the collapse of democracy of America and its venerated position in the world. This cannot be, must not be! This cannot stand even if it takes a hand from heaven - reaching down to intervene.

We've heard many times before, power corrupts and absolute power corrupts absolutely. Seventy seven percent of America is now asking what were you all thinking? To whom were you giving allegiance to do his bidding when you have commited to work for the people for whom you are bound by oath to serve? We are the citizens of these United States! Do you not remember us? We The People? We are your bosses - you cannot be influenced to blindly follow some Svengali!

It is unfathomable how you can live with yourselves, much less with your families and friends! Look in the mirror. Look at yourselves! How can you stand yourselves? How can you face your families? How can you face your children when

84   they know better than you what damage you may have done to the American constitution of this wonderful place. A place in which they, by your inaction, someday, may be required to live in and may have nothing of value to live for!

NO one should have such power. Not anyone. No one must be above the law, not even the Resident of the United States. So many of us, such a majority of us, feel that you need to take a very hard look at yourselves and get a firm grip on what has always been right for America. Do your job - you took an oath to work for us and defend the United States. Now just do it!

Oh, Moscow Mitch. You seem to stand up for Putin's ultimate destruction of America. You must be so very proud! You stood up there so proud like a peacock. You seemed to imply that you were in control; could do anything. You can do it all and will do it all and they just cannot stop you, no matter how totally valid their evidence is or is presented. Just let them try.

Whoever heard of any trial in America where the jury foreman runs the trial, much less coordinates trial strategy with the defendant? The jury foreman works for the court, not the person on trial! That's no trial. That's a sham trial! Well, as Goliath found out, 'Pride goeth before the fall.' 'The bigger they are, the harder they fall.' May we soon all hope to take comfort from these Words.

GOP Senators: What can you possibly tell your 12 year old son or daughter when they know you voted to not only ignore overly compelling evidence that might save this nation from possible national security risks but possibly condemn this nation to a path to a dictatorship. Do you know? Have you ever really stopped a moment - like in Church - to seriously think about it? When have you ever really taken it to heart?

Here is quite an intriguing thought! When you unleash the glint of the brandishing sword, you are never quite sure where it goes, where it is going to come back, where it will land or what it might slay. You may actually be mounting your heads on your own pikes by becoming the victims of this apparent, senseless abdication of Justice: the diminishing of America that has seemingly been unleashed. This may very well come back to bite you all in the proverbial butt!

There must be an epitaph for this. I can't quite figure out what it is. But, by God, we have come to such a terrible place in such a short time, we must have hope that there is a way to get better and get much better very soon and do it completely.

*Author's updated note: Things have so dramatically changed in just the past 2 months with the now deadly onslaught of the Covid 19 virus that the Impeachment trial is almost totally forgotten. It is unthinkable to suggest that Heaven has sent it but, biblically speaking, is that not what is often implied in the 'Book' when pestilences are described or discussed?   For Example:

Deuteronomy 32:24
They shall be wasted with hunger, and devoured by plague and poisonous pestilence; I will send the teeth of beasts against them, with the venom of things that crawl in the dust.

or

Ezekiel 14:19
Or suppose I were to pour out my Fury by sending an epidemic into the land, and the disease killed people and animals alike.

CHAPTER 24
The HONOR and REPUTATION of AMERICA

There was a time when people in the United States valued the reputation and honor of the United States - both here at home and around the world. We were the beacon of Democracy and a fountain of generally honorable images and perceptions. Our word was trusted, as well as treaties that were considered binding. We could be trusted to not arbitrarily renege on a treaty or suddenly decide that now we don't think it's right and just cancel it unilaterally.

So what we have seen in the past 3 years is the cancellation of the Paris Climate Accords, the JCPOA denuclearization agreement with Iran, NAFTA with Mexico and Canada and the Trans-Pacific trade agreement. That's just the tip of the iceberg. By derogatory rhetoric, our relationships with our allies around the world, and in particular, NATO, have been severely undermined. Our world image and prestige are very much in jeopardy. As a result, the world leaders tend to now be looking to Russia and China for guidance and alliances.

So what does this mean? In just three short years, our Role - as the beacon to the world for Democracy and a world leader - seems to have plummeted and been severely damaged - hopefully not irreversibly. Actions - as seen implemented nationally and worldwide - are, or are nearly, irreversible. Our Institutions that supported us so ably for years, have been so completely diminished, under-staffed, underfunded and under -managed - by appointees - not approved by Congress - may have become mere skeletons of themselves. Traditions - that have regulated us and have maintained this democracy - have seemingly been ignored, set aside or just outright eliminated. Apparently, these very detrimental things have been totally normalized - making them very hard to reinstate.

What do we do? Whatever do we do? Another 4 years of this and there could be absolutely no going back. In fact the changes are now so rapid in a certain direction that in far less than 4 years this democracy could be so totally changed into something entirely different - something that may not be so pleasant or desirable. 300 million people would suddenly have to find someplace else to live and something else to do. There's no way that anyone who has lived here even 10 years would want to live under a new regime or direction like that.

I just heard the extremely disturbing news that the justice department may be trying to enact changes to citizens' right laws such as - Writ of Habeas Corpus - that fundamentally were to secure freedoms and our rights. This is seemingly done under the premise of enacting emergency laws justified by the Covid 19 virus pandemic. I've heard that there was a lot of that going around in Europe - mid 40's - and in other countries which we now consider under less than desirable regimes.

Emergency laws are supposed to be laws that revert back when the emergency is over, but history has pretty much shown that once the law gets installed - depending upon the administration at the time - they may just forget to change it back and it could become a permanent part of the new way of life. These things tend to happen way too often, especially if a new authoritarian government just might have been formed.

Habeas Corpus is an important part of the Constitution. The Constitution specifically includes the Habeas clause in the Suspension Clause (Clause 2) located in Article one, Section 9. It states, 'The privilege of the Writ of Habeas Corpus shall not be suspended, unless when in cases of rebellion or invasion the public safety may require it.'   Enough Said?!

The ENEMIES LIST and the DARK STATE

We now **turn to 'enemies lists'. It's rumored the Resident may have been working on them - perhaps since before the impeachment proceedings started. From the beginning, three years ago, he's been talking about the Deep Dark State. Those are the people who have been 'purposely left behind' in key positions by the previous administration to prevent the new Resident or the party in charge to accomplish their goals.**

If you ever doubted that the Resident might be tied to Putin by a tether or by the hip - you might just kiss that doubt away right now. By these two terms it might be confirmed that this connection may go back at least to 2015. These two terms are directly from a dictator's playbook - possibly like Putin's Playbook. These two terms are just never ever used in a democracy like the United States - not ever! They are an anathema to a well-functioning democracy and totally alien to its ability to remain as a democracy. They are only used by dictators of 3rd or 4th World countries - by people who want to rule absolutely and control every source of resistance to a dictator or to a dictator's government. Just Not Done "."

Dictators use this kind of thinking. A dictator uses tactics like these as applied directly to members of the government to control allegiance and totally root out dissidence. When you hear a head of state yell out at rallies, 'lock her up' about someone who ran against him as a candidate - you know that it is absolutely not what is done in any well-run democracy. '.'

We do not lock up our rivals in a Democracy. We do not belittle or abuse our rivals in our Democracy. We do not harass and criminally investigate our rivals in our democracy. This is criminality - a Crime Boss kind of thinking and tactic.

It is also used very effectively by autocratic dictators in 3rd World countries. We do not run criminal investigations on people who were just doing the jobs they were elected to do or selected to do by elected officials. You just do not do this to normal law-abiding and functioning citizens - our servants.

Now to the Deep State. What I just said above, leads right into this nonsense about a Deep State. A democracy is based on three branches of government; the judicial, the administrative and the legislative branches which are equal in stature and authority and have responsibilities to act as a check and balance against the other branches. Particularly used, in this case, for the executive branch or the executive himself.

Part of the stability of this kind of government, a Democracy, is that people are hired into Bureaus, Agencies and offices, such as the FBI and Intelligence, to do various long-term kinds of work using their skills to protect the nation and its people from Foreign or Domestic crimes or harm. These people are career people. They are there for a very long time by design to be the stable part of the government when politics changes. They are the non-political experts who know their job and do their job very well - carrying it out regardless of who the president is or who is in Congress or who's in the Courts. That gives democracy it's ultimate stability to operate over long periods independently of the whims of the moment.

So when a leader at the top of the government starts claiming that people that have been doing their jobs - are committing espionage or being part of a Dark State trying to take down the Resident or the administration or the government - you feel that you may now be living under a dictatorship. No road map. It is just common sense. You just know that. That is Never Done in a democracy such as the United States.

90   So when you hear it - look out - you may have crossed over from a democracy. By then, to reverse it may be very very difficult. Even an election may not be successful at ridding the country of such an entity that has metastasized to that point. Hopefully, we may not be at that point quite yet!

Did no-one look into this man's background before he ran for office or was Selected? Did no one know the kinds of things he did in business or the kind of people he was associated with in business or dealings he had, for example, with Putin before being Selected? Why wouldn't we have done much more Due Diligence as we would have done before selecting a president of a small company in any town in the US? Would we ever consider a con man to be the head of the government of the United States? Would we ever consider a person with seemingly full intent to destroy the United States? I mean completely. So much seemingly doing so, and seems well on the way to completing it right before our very eyes?

Every American should be able to recognize similar behavior from movies they've seen. The people of America should be able to recognize the characteristics of dictators from other countries. Red flags should have been seen by experts, and they should have warned us this might be someone that may be truly on the wrong path for America. Why isn't there a published road map going into an election which sends up red flags when these things are suspected? When Intelligence experts may have seen these flags, why wasn't an alarm set off immediately? Oh yes, I forgot, many of those experts are the people that are being *investigated right now*!

WITNESS TAMPERING and INTIMIDATION
and MANIPULATION of PROSECUTORS

You say any of these things anywhere near a courtroom in the United States and you're bound to have trouble in a trial - possibly ending in at least a mistrial or a lot of other crimes and offenses that will be thrown at you. None of these things are considered to be petty offenses in a courtroom or a trial of any kind or at any level or stature of a court. This kind of crime is just not taken lightly and quite often deserves quite a number of years of incarceration for just this or similar offenses alone. It often might be associated with gang or organized crime trials.

In a recent trial, these were some of the indictments for which Mr. Stone was found guilty in a federal court. The federal incarceration guidelines apparently were 7 to 9 years for these offenses. The Resident apparently thought they should be much less. Seemingly, the Attorney General stepped in to alter the recommendations to the court to be much less time. Far worse, he has apparently now stepped in to try to drop charges against someone who may have committed serious crimes against the state. That person confessed in court at least twice to those crimes and was only awaiting sentencing.

Now I ask you. How does that represent the people's interests for Justice in our federal courts or in the DOJ's office? That same Attorney General had just recently stated that the DOJ should throw maximum sentences at crimes prosecuted in federal courts. Apparently, the conclusion is that maximum sentences are good enough for Joe Blow but not for friends or buddies of people in high places. Nothing seems good enough for them even if it might be zero time in jail. What happened to 'no one is above the law' in the United States of America?

92   What happened to 'equal justice under the law'? What happened to 'not being able to buy your way out of a sentence for a crime' if you had enough money or influence? Apparently it's screwing the little guy who doesn't seem to have the money. It might appear, corruption abounds in this present administration! If you believed the swamp was drained - you might discover that they filled it with Alligators.

Every day, more and more, we may be seeing the real results of the Selection of a Resident that was probably the worst possible thing that could happen to America in its entire history. The worst part is it's not over. The worst part is we are just now beginning to see how really bad it is and how much worse it may get before it is hopefully ended by this coming election.

Oh yes, we are not quite through with this chapter. There is this nasty little matter of manipulation of prosecutors. How independent is this Attorney General that is at the head of our DOJ - the people's Department of Justice? It seems that we had a very independent group of Justice prosecutors in DC and a particularly independent group of prosecutors in the southern district of New York. Both of these groups have been working to investigate a number of people who, in one way or another, were apparently involved in meddling in the election in 2016 or somehow possibly related to activities in Russia trying to influence the outcome of the 2016 election.

There were apparently 11 or 12 of these cases being investigated as a result of the Mueller investigation into activities related to Russian involvement in the 2016 election. These two prosecuting offices are well known for their total independence and their fairness in evidence collection.

Apparently, this same Attorney General - supposedly the People's Attorney General to provide Equal Justice for the United States - has intervened in these Justice Departments to meddle with those in charge of these investigations in a way that they might be severely compromised - if not totally shut down. It would seem that the outcome of this effort is to bury these and the entire existence of the Mueller report along with Russia's involvement concerning the 2016 election - apparently so that it will no longer be in existence. Finito!

Again, one has only to ask this very basic question. Why is it so damn important to obliterate the very existence of the Mueller report when it presumably had been declared by the Attorney General to exonerate the Resident completely of any involvement with Russia or in it's meddling with the 2016 election to favor the selection of this Resident to that office?

Only a guilty person would attempt to try to destroy all evidence of any guilt - and that report has more than enough evidence to adequately justify a strong connection to Russia in the 2016 election. These actions alone seem enough to verify that connection. Why are we not able to do what detectives do with a storyboard? Making connections with string from one suspect to another to critically show how these groups of people were interconnected to take actions to pull off the Selection of the Resident with the aid of Russian involvement? All of the evidence that was collected by US and international news seemed more effective by far than the Mueller report at connecting the dots. Sadly, that report seemed nearly a total waste of time, money and in particular the total waste of two precious years that seriously irritated the Resident, but prevented real progress in discovery and possible important needed action. That was no way to run an election in the United States of America! NO WAY! NO HOW!

CHAPTER 27
SVENGALI, ROBESPIERRE and F. A. MESMER

Three very interesting early personages that all have some bearing upon some of the ideas developed in this book. I added them here for your brief intermission, a respite and a very hearty retrospection and personal reflection.

Svengali is a fictional character in George du Maurier's 1895 novel <u>Trilby</u>. Svengali is a musician who seduces, dominates and exploits Trilby, a young Irish girl and makes her a famous singer..

The word Svengali has come to refer to a person who, with evil intent, dominates, manipulates and controls another. In court, a Svengali defense is a legal tactic that purports the defendant to be a pawn in the scheme of a greater and more influential criminal mastermind.

F. A. MESMER A therapeutic system of healing by Mesmer - a technique to induce a trance. Mesmer was a person who used an induced trance to control or have mesmeric influence on another, possibly for a sinister purpose. See e.g. 'mesmerize'.

Maximilian Robespierre: Often quoted Quotes. These are very enlightening and very interesting to read. I very much think that they will play in your mind as applied to this book.

*A nation is truly corrupted when having... lost its character and its liberty, it passes from democracy to aristocracy or to monarchy. That is the decrepitude and death of the body politic...

*The Secret of Freedom lies in educating people, whereas the secret of tyranny is in keeping them ignorant.

*The king must die so that the country can live.

*To punish the oppressors of humanity is clemency; to forgive them is cruelty.

*Again it may be said, that to love justice and equality the people need no great effort for virtue; it is sufficient that they love themselves.

*Any institution which does not suppose the people are good, and the magistrate corruptible, is evil.

*The general 'will' rules in society as the private 'will' governs each individual.

*Crime butchers innocence to secure a throne, and innocence struggles with all its might against the attempts of crime.

*Atheism is aristocratic; the idea of a great Being that watches over oppressed innocence and punishes triumphant crime is altogether popular.

*Any law which violates the inalienable rights of man is essentially unjust and tyrannical; it is not a law at all.

*Softness to Traitors will destroy us all.

*Peoples do not judge in the same way as courts of law; they do not hand down sentences, they throw thunderbolts; they do not condemn Kings, they drop them back into the void; and this justice is worth just as much as that of the courts.

*One can... never create freedom by an invading force.

*We must smother the internal and external enemies of the Republic or perish with it; now in this situation, the first maxim of our policy ought to be to lead the People by reason and the People's enemies by terror.

*Smuggle out the truth, pass it through all the obstacles that its enemies fabricate; multiply, spread by all means possible her message so that she may triumph

*Through zeal and civic action - counterbalance the influence of money and the machinations lavished on the propagation of deception. That, in my opinion, is the most useful activity in the most sacred duty of pure patriotism.

96   *Men of all countries are brothers, and the different people should help one another to the best of their ability, like citizens of the same state.

*It is in time of war that the executive power displays the most redoubtable energy and that it wields a sort of dictatorship most ominous to a nascent Liberty...

*War is always the first object of a powerful government which wishes to increase its power. I shall not speak to you of the opportunity that a war affords for a government to exhaust the people and to dissipate its treasure and to cover with an impenetrable veil its depredations and its errors...

*Equality of Rights is established by Nature; Society, far from impairing it, guarantees it against the abuse of power which renders it illusory.

*The people ask only for what is necessary, it only wants justice and tranquility. The rich aspire to everything, they want to invade and dominate everything.

*Abuses are the work and the domain of the rich, they are the scourges of the people: the interest of the people is the general interest, that of the rich is a particular interest.

*It has been said that terror is the principle of despotic government. Does your government therefore resemble despotism?

*Yes, as the sword that gleams in the hands of the heroes of Liberty resembles that with which the henchmen of tyranny are armed.

*I utter this deadly truth with regret, but Louis must die, because the homeland must live.

*The most extravagant idea that can be born in the head of a political thinker is to believe that it suffices for people to enter, weapons in hand, among a foreign people and expect to have it's laws and constitution embraced. No one loves armed missionaries; the first lesson of nature and prudence is to repulse them as enemies.

*In every country where nature provides for the needs of
men with prodigality, scarcity can only be imputed to defects of administration or of the laws themselves; bad laws and bad administration have their origins in false principles and bad morals.

*The right to punish the tyrant and the right to dethrone him are the same thing; both include the same forms. The tyrant's trial is the insurrection; the verdict, the collapse of his power; the sentence, whatever the liberty of the people requires.

*Happily virtue is natural in the people, despite aristocratic prejudices.

*We wish, in a word, to fulfill the intentions of nature and the destiny of man, realize the promises of philosophy, and I acquit providences of a long reign of crime and tyranny.

*So that France may become the model for all nations, the terror of oppressors, the consolation of the oppressed. That is our ambition, that is our goal.

*Citizens, did you want a revolution without Revolution?

*Food that is necessary for man's existence is as sacred as life itself. Everything that is indispensable for its preservation is the common property of society as a whole. It is only the surplus that is private property and can be safely left to individual commercial enterprises.

*What is a person who, among men equal in rights, dares to declare his fellows unworthy of theirs, and to take them away for his own advantage! Amen. We sure understand this one!

There is just so much in these - complete, brilliant wisdom in all of his quotes that - written during the French Revolution - have so much to bear on our present situation and issues. I sincerely hope that you all perceived the poignancy of sheer knowledge displayed in these simple short pearls of wisdom. In a very real sense these condensed thoughts were written in similar times and during periods of similar stressful actions.

CHAPTER 28
DECENT PEOPLE BEING TRANSFORMED

What breadth or depth of mesmerism does it take to convert a decent person into the evil spawning person that they represent? What does it take to clone a decent person into being a fawning, evil doppelganger, mirror image, lackey of an evil criminal host? It must take complete alchemy!

In short, throughout these three years, we have seen people - decent people - politicians, people of honor, grace and intelligence - discerning intellects and critically thinking people, seemingly become Jekyll and Hydes. Unfortunately, they seem to permanently end up as Mr. Hyde. And in this role they would remain damned for the rest of their lives. What is worse, seemingly in these cases, there is no cure for these transformations. They have apparently become the clones of the master that they seemingly chose to follow.

For the majority of those who live in these United States who themselves are decent discerning people and have known these people before being cloned, cannot comprehend -- cannot imagine how these people that they have known for decades have become something that they do not recognize nor can they understand their current behavior.

It all goes well beyond any concept of logic or reasoning. It just cannot be described or understood by anything that our common decent people have contemplated, understood, or can imagine. How could this happen?

There's one that is an extreme case in point! He used to have, (for a Republican) liberal views and drew rational conclusions about events whether on national security or political issues or events. He could be counted on to come up with reasonable evaluations of critical situations and be pretty much on the sane side of crisis issues as well as day-to-day policies.   One golf game. Just one game and he seemingly became a very irrational, confusing person that we see today.

Every time I see him talk on television in response to a crucial issue or pronouncements or actions that have agitated, I think to myself, does this guy ever look at himself on TV? Does he ever listen to what he's now saying? Would it ever make sense to him? Why is he not horrified, ashamed, besmirched or disgraced by his pronouncements? Look at yourself on television, man! What do you see? Can you actually stand there and not throw a brick at the television set? Not be horrified by the very things you are saying totally in antithesis of your former reasonable self? My God man, get a real life! At least get back to who you were before you were cloned by the body snatchers.   ------------Please don't forget this DAY!----------
EXTREMELY IMPORTANT DAY: {June 1, 2020} Perhaps the most destructive day in the life of the Democracy of the United States of America. * God help us that it will not become one of the most pivotally disastrous days - one that will be totally destructive of our future freedoms and life as we know it. The Resident, today, either did or threatened to impose the Insurrection Act of 1807- thus also the Posse Comitatus Act of 1878 which limits the use of federal military personel to enforce domestic policies against the citizens of the U.S. 'If a city or state refuses to take actions necessary to defend life and property of their residents, then I will deploy the United States Military and quickly solve the problem for them.' This could be the fast road to Nationalism. _Important_: The Resident called Putin the morning of 6/1/20 and among other things apparently wanted to invite him to rejoin the G7. He was also in contact with Putin on March 30, April 9, 10, 12, 25 and 5/7/20

CHAPTER 29
WHO WERE THEY before EPIPHANY?

The events of the last several weeks, since the acquittal in the impeachment, have shown an emboldenment of the Resident in ways so completely unimaginable to anybody in America that we must, by force, cry out in fear for what may be coming next. It seems so unbelievable! I have only to refer to the chapter of the Resident's visits to Kim and Putin to get a feel of how dire and unimaginable these possibilities could be if possibly tutored by these two rascals. The 'horror' of what might have been achieved by these visits gives a feel to what I'm just about to discuss.

Who were these people that were once GOP politicians, Congressmen or Senators? Did they grow up pretty much normally but some time, perhaps in high school, realized that 'when I grow up I want to be a fascist or a russian bolshevik'? 'That's what I really want to be.' However, in the meantime until the right person comes along, 'I'm going to be a politician and I'm going to be a constitutionalist and I'm going to get elected to represent those who put me in office.' 'I'm going to represent their needs for schools, better economies, more available jobs, lower unemployment and all of those great things.' 'I'm going to fight for and pledge to defend the Constitution and defend the rule of law to keep this nation great, safe and most of all - Democratic.'

So what happens when a person who seemingly is a bumbling fool, has no knowledge of or cares to have any knowledge of the Constitution and doesn't believe in the rule of law -- takes over the minds of these GOP clones as if by a mind warp? I mean, were they latent fascists, bolsheviks in their subconscious youths? I mean did they have, deep down, hidden dispositions to be this kind of odd minded GOP?

The Resident seemingly doesn't believe that he needs the Congress or the courts - except to sue people. Why is it that these people, who presumably at one time grew up, as the rest of us did, believing in the Constitution, the rule of law, a democratic way of life, seemingly suddenly choose to take this different path? How could it happen, when they lived in a place that was run by the rule of law that insured, to the best of its ability, peace, tranquility and prosperity?

Why now, are they seemingly all acting as if somewhere in their deep dark past and dreams they perhaps really wanted to be bolsheviks who wanted to take over our rule of law Democracy? After they, or their families, have lived here, perhaps, for generations - why might they seemingly be inclined to want to turn it into a Russian style dictatorship - requiring total loyalty as the only means of keeping their jobs? Why be in an environment where if one steps out of line - somebody else, that may be far worse, steps in?

My first question is; 'where in hell do they find the next person that could be worse?' Where do *they* come from? What country did they live in before they were so dissatisfied with the rule of law and the Constitution that they are so eager to give it all up and join this form of seeming insanity?

Where? Where in hell would anybody, after a normal time in grade school, high school or college and into politics, have latent tendencies to be fascists or bolsheviks just waiting to come out? I can't understand how these people can suddenly have such an awful, awful epiphany and seemingly embrace it as if this is what they always wanted to be all their lives! I don't think so. OMG! They have children who know better. They have grandchildren who know better! Where in Hell have they been hiding? Where in Hell have these alter egos been hiding?

102   Where were those in the 40's, when fascism rose to power, that suddenly arose to do the bidding and dirty work? It is said that every deviant, derelict, dysfunctional sociopath in society was ready to join and be part of the government. Apparently, in every society, there must be some sort of bell curve of behaviors and at the very bottom of the bell curve are the scum of the earth. The totally out-of-sorts people with deep, hidden grudges against Society. How did they survive?

They were people without morals - without any moral code whatsoever. They had no empathy for anyone - they are total societal misfits - barely surviving within a normal functioning democracy. These people are relegated to the dark corners of humanity - hidden away and minimized and marginalized to the point where they sort of just barely existed.

What happened was, these people were found - and given not only Authority but Power -- all that they needed. That is all they needed to come forth and do whatever they felt like doing because they could get by with it and be rewarded for it. They could do no wrong. They had been given a free hand to be the meanest bastards you would never want to meet. The meaner they were the better, because by being a mean bastard you struck fear in normal people's hearts. It was such a dark fear that if you didn't fall in line you'd be killed. There was no other alternative. Life had no consequence!

Well, the last two weeks have shown us that we may be at that point now in America. If you are going to be part of this man's government you have to absolutely swear an oath - not to the United States of America or to the Constitution. If you have the misfortune to work in this government and you fall out of line - you may be toast. If in your job you happen to tell the truth and it isn't liked - you may no longer have your job and worse,

you might be persecuted or prosecuted. You might be
called a criminal against the State - a traitor that may have committed treason.

You may be identified as part of the Deep State - planted there by the previous occupiers so that they could help destroy the new kingdom. It is just damn hard to fathom how any person could just become one of those sycophants that just seems to be so overly supportive of this regime. Where's the soul?

There is so much we needed to know closer to the beginning - things not familiar to us here in America. In history it has too often been shown that early knowledge was mandatory in order to mitigate impending situations that followed. Visible hidden evidence only became all too clear - all too late to do much remediation. It is no surprise that someone who might be, for whatever reason, trying to pull some fast one on the public, would do all they can to keep it absolutely secret and out of sight. I don't think we have been disappointed in this case by this seemingly ever present behavior.

Eventually it begins to become clear you can see definite things through the smoke screen that are very disturbing. Clear indications that, a year or two before, you should have seen and taken swift action to mitigate. Some of this is happening with the virus pandemic that we are now fighting. Some didn't pay attention to known facts and virus dynamics. Instead of swift action they seemed prone to slow foot dragging. There are so many dire lessons - that we must seriously heed in the future. Has it already become too late?

Before the final steps of publishing this book I awoke from my sleep with the essence of an epilogue to summarize what I had discovered while writing this book. All of these various and seemingly varied chapters - suddenly coalesced into one conglomerate - a very profound thought - perhaps a synopsis.

We find ourselves in a horrible global pandemic of a brand new virus to which no one is immune. This is so dangerous that, like the 1918 Spanish Flu, a significant part of the world population could die - 3% to 5% - if not mitigated by as swift, decisive and effective actions as possible. The Bubonic plague deaths were estimated at 30% to 60% of the world population. They knew so much less about such things then.

The Epiphany, as revealed by the summation of the book, was in effect a different kind of global pandemic that appears to be sweeping many parts of the world today. We have seen its essence in the recent elections in the EU, France, England (with Brexit), Turkey, Italy, etc.. Nationist movements, such as those seemingly sweeping Europe, as Marine Le Pen, won out 24% over Macron's 21% in France in recent EU elections. This Populist, Nationist, Progressive movement seemingly is more prevalent now here, as in other parts of the world. While fascism is often rooted in Populism it doesn't mean that Populism always ends in fascism.

As stated earlier, a viral pandemic acts like an atomic bomb - a basic chain reaction. The bomb occurs in milliseconds. The viral pandemic - much slower - takes a few to many months to play out - at least the first time. The Nationalist Populism pandemic, however, plays out over a period of several years. Boron absorbers can slow the reaction in the atomic reactor - while distancing is most important to slow a viral pandemic.

So what is available to slow the onslaught of the Populist, Nationalist, Progressive worldwide movements? First of all these are ideology driven - not inanimate objects like Uranium atoms or viruses. Neither of those two have minds or can think or remember prior events or be convinced of or imagine other circumstances. As a result, they tend to follow laws of physics or human nature.

The latter can only be influenced by words - ie, education, propaganda or verbal persuasion of the mind and emotions. These radical ideas just seem to be so counterintuitive to common sense, basic human needs and desires that little to nothing could possibly overwhelm them. However, lies, false words - propaganda are very effective at overcoming these natural instincts. That is what makes this pandemic so very dangerous - when even human instincts and common sense can be overwhelmed. So how can one slow or stop such a dangerous runaway train? There-in lies the 'fight to control human minds'. Lies, fake news, alternate truths, deceit and propaganda are mainsprings of these kinds of movements. Kitch, catchy slogans, appeal to an ad hoc patriotism. Simple phrases like 'Lock her up' 'build the wall' 'who will pay for it?' that can be easily remembered and chanted - all add to a cohesiveness leading to a kind of cultism which might be characterized as similar to 'Jonestown'. I'm patiently waiting for my 'kool-aid'. When do we get our 'kool-aid', please?

The moderator to this kind of chain reaction? That's a hard one. Since words - primarily lies - are the propagators - then it must be words - THE TRUTH - that has to be used to slow it down or possibly reverse it. But how do you force THE TRUTH into closed minds? How do you find a crack into the psyche of a cultist member? I've tried to find answers in the literature and found it sadly bereft. Pervasive truth checking?

106   Often much of what has spurred the rise of Nationalism Is an apparent mistrust of liberal thinking parties that have seemingly abandoned the working class in favor of Wall street over main street. In effect they seem to have offered little for ordinary working people and have failed to mitigate rapidly increasing inequality. The rich get richer while the poor get poorer. So the simplest methods to counter or diminish Nationalism seems to be to promote a progressive agenda that would definitely side with working people again.

Those 70,000 votes that Selected the one in the White House were from typically liberal leaning - known as rust belt - states that apparently may have felt ignored by the liberal party. They expressed their possible anger in a protest vote against the usual party by voting for someone who often chided them with: 'what have you got to lose?'. And by adding a catchy phrase of 'Making America Great Again' - typically a Nationlist kind of sentiment - especially for those who may have seriously felt left behind by their historically supportive party!

Right now we must counter an incredibly ineffective, flawed, administration that seems to think like a rogue 10K marathon runner. He starts the race with the others - then ducks out - catches a ride to the finish line neighborhood - and jumps out in front of those dedicated, hard working, disciplined racers to cross the finish line just before them. That is equivalent to doing nothing during the 2 most critical months of the virus. Then only after the nation's governors, out of necessity, have done all that they could to mitigate it. He then steps in and asserts that he and the do nothing federal government have been heroic in fighting this virus! What a total pile of BS!

To counter this kind of Nationistic bull shit is simply TRUTH and progressive agendas to benefit the forgotten workers.

Oh my God, oh my GOD! All of the muted and subtle warnings that I made in this book - were just about to be sent to the publisher when things happened in just the last two or three days that would make the Democratic citizen's - rule of law, Constitution defending - mind literally explode! So much so that I had to add at least two more pages to this book as a dire warning that must be heeded as soon as possible. Act NOW!

Large groups of Constitution, rule of law and democracy - minded people cannot afford to idly talk about aspirations any more. They must immediately get together to form groups or institutions that will formulate and take decisive actions now. We can no longer 'pray for the families of Sandy Hook kids' and do nothing! The time has come for serious intervention and dire mitigation on a scale no less important than the one that should have been put in place for this world threatening pandemic. We can no longer pray for something to happen - real urgent action must be taken now to save this Nation - especially before the election. That's how bad things are and they are very rapidly moving to become far WORSE!

Way too often I hear news people and especially politicians, utter 'Well, this is awful - somebody should do something' or 'Oh, that's just the way he is'! NO! Never, EVER under any circumstances do you make excuses or allowences for bad, totally destructive behavior. I don't give a DAMN who he is!

Let's review steps often taken by a would-be autocrat hell bent upon the gradual take over of a well running democracy.

1. Obliterate the validity of the free press and news media - that had been the first fundamental necessary part of a democracy - or just take it over or censure it thoroghly.

2. Replace the Head of the DOJ with a person that is totally loyal and that will effectively weaponize it against your opponents or perceived enemies and will do everything to encourage the end of the rule of law. Your loyalists!

3. Stack the courts with loyalist cronies who may not even be real or effective judges. In effect, they may have taken loyalty oaths to you. This is by far the most anti Democratic thing that you can do. This is never, ever done in a functioning Democracy!

4. Always Lie! This way no one can ever convict you based upon facts said!   When based upon Lies - America dies!

5. Stack the house (or convert them) that is responsible for approving all of your appointees (including judges) and will block all of the People's legislation and approve of only your hand picked laws and expressions.

6. Fill all cabinet positions with handpicked Department Cronies that will do your bidding to administratively demolish the real effectiveness of those adminstrations from protecting your bosses, ie. the American citizens, from poluted water, air and environments - bad food or drugs - homeland security - pestilence, plagues and wars.

7. Pick a Secretary of State whose agenda is foremost to look out for your own financial, business and political interests - and thereby act upon them on your behalf and to your favor. This is just not done in a Democracy.

8. Censure all scientists from crucial areas affecting the ultimate well being of the people, such as in health, economics, climate change or environmental issues.

9. Remove all Inspector Generals that may or do have jurisdiction over possible acts of corruption or law that may affect you or your Cronies directly.

Look at these. Are we not already in deep Doo Doo? Act Now!

The United States, and the entire world, find ourselves trying to fight and survive one of the deadliest worldwide viral pandemics in over 100 years - since the 1918 Spanish Flu. In this severe crisis when it would be expected that our Federal Government would have mobilized to do everything that was possible to save our nation from getting infected or more importantly to prevent unneeded deaths - we appear to come up woefully short to what appears to be severe foot dragging.

Where *'expected to serve'* is the norm, the opposite seems to be the intent. Where the immediate financial needs of an entire vulnerable population are paramount - huge corporations and the rich seem to be highly served to the detriment of the most vulnerable. When the most vulnerable are at risk: retirement communities, prisons, high density food processing plants and minority people and neighborhoods seem to have the highest infection rates and densities and seem to be served the least of all - seemingly deliberately ignored and forgotten!

Most disturbing of all is that during this extremely serious crisis we find, apparently purposeful foot dragging and much of what's been depicted in 1. to 9. above, detrimentally going on in the background with an apparently deliberate force.

Not to diminish its import or impact, we as a nation seem to now have faux militias storming into our state legislative houses and chambers armed with automatic long guns and intimidating legislators and spectators. This only happens in autocratic third world countries - never in the very beacon of Democracy - the United States of America. Where are those GOP constitutionalists that till now have so fervently defended the precepts of the Constitution and the rule of law? Is this not understood to be what happens near the end of a democracy such as in Europe in the '30s? Are we already there? Hmm?

110　　Life and its meaning or, perversely - lack of meaning, has taken on so many new shapes, colors and dimensions. Not only with the Pandemic - but so many other things have been thrust to the forefront of attention such as *Black Lives Matter.* This is as the result of an unprecedented number of deaths of either seemingly innocent blacks or blacks with minor infractions at the hands of police by either being shot for no reason or choke holds with knees or arms of policemen. A characteristic seems to be that it occurs even after the victim (like George Floyd in Minneapolis) cries out that he can't breath over and over again - cries that seemingly go totally unheeded by the perpetrator until he is found dead after 8 minutes and 46 seconds.

These events have resulted in civil demonstrations all over the United States as well as the world and are continuing today - more than a month later. These peaceful demonstrations are populated with not just blacks but caucasians and other ethnicities as well. The administration is apparently trying to redirect to the support of *law and order* rather than systemic racism that is seemingly included in our nationwide policing environments as well as many other parts of our society such as banks, housing, jobs, neighborhoods, life and income.

This is at least a 240 year old problem - perhaps much longer - but never ever seems to get solved despite a number of similar incidents that have brought it to the fore in past years. Attempts to do something about this have in general failed. This pandemic and in particular this very administration have seemingly set the conditions for this time to have so much more meaning to a very much expanded segment of our - and world - population. Hopefully, more significant action will be taken to make meaningful improvements this time. Much is being done at State and City levels as we are going to press.

This response by the administration is also being seen
as a stark indicator of not only the inadequacies of their
response but also a stark measure of the demonstrated lack of
empathy for extremely dire human circumstances. 20 to 45
million Americans have been thrust out of work in a very short
period of time by this worldwide viral pandemic. Most of those
live, paycheck to paycheck. Several attempts by congress -
not the Resident - set up monetary programs to try to alleviate
this problem - albeit - to a limited few affected people and for
far too short a time to sustain them for the length of time that
this virus is going to keep them from full or even temporary
employment.

One thing has become very apparent as we watch action in the
House and Senate. Almost without exception, when the
Republicans get up to speak on the floor or in a hearing on the
subject, they tend to find ways to block any humanitarian
efforts or means to a meaningful stimulus or support that will
not only ease the present burden of those who employ them -
the people of the United States - but more importantly would
dramatically increase the prospect of a bigger, healthier and
sooner recovery for all - businesses included. The Dems, on
the other hand, seem to be working to aid people through the
crisis - that is not of their making - and will most definitely
shorten the burden till a recovery that will make that eventual
result so much more effective and complete. The Republicans
seem to always be so totally reactionary and contradictory -
often obfuscating the real problem and the means to best
address it and eventually fix it. One has the feeling that if
scientists learned that a meteor would be hitting the world -
the GOP would be finding ways to justify it as a Hoax or a plot
against the administration. I.e. just the opposite of reality.
They would be finding ways to blame someone or some other
group of trying to put a fast one over on them and the nation.

112   Speaking of Hoax, have you all noticed a pattern that has become prevalent over four years? The word Hoax seems to predictably deflect from what is the truth to some other place.

Fake news is a Hoax. The Russia connection is a Hoax. The COVID 19 virus and pandemic is a Hoax. (See pages 61, 63 and 69) The results of the Mueller report are a Hoax. I know that each of you will be able to recollect and count perhaps a dozen more examples that I have forgotten - but the pattern is by now extremely clear. Anything that seems threatening or perhaps very close to the "truth" suddenly is labeled a Hoax! It is a clumsy attempt at "deflection". It's like in a game of poker, a player starts to hum or do a particular motion, those in the know, are aware that he knows that he has a very BAD hand.

In this regard, we have a duzy. The news has pretty well been documented and more than alleges that Russia through the G.R.U. was paying bounties thru the Taliban to kill American and Allied forces. The Resident recently called the "reports" a Hoax. There first were excuses of not knowing anything about it even though several credible sources say that it was in his late February, 2020 PDB. The implications of this whole story and the numerous contexts upon which it is bound are very disturbing to most Americans, especially military families and those patriotic to military endeavors such as Senators and Congressmen - particularly of the Republican persuasion.

This story has many detrimental implications that affect the Resident. If he did know about this heinous bounty, why didn't he take decisive action to do something about it in those 5 or 6 calls with Putin in late March - June 1st? If he didn't know about it, as first claimed, then he or someone in line was clearly derelict in not being on top of the dire consequences. This story has multiple, unfavorable consequences. All BAD!

Talk to any political scientist of any persuasion or bent and they will all tell you that a leader at the top of a nation that has ENEMY LISTS is not the leader of a Democracy or anything resembling a Democracy! They are either dictators or soon to be dictators / monarchs of a third or fourth world, second rate country! They are certainly not the leader of a country that they promised "TO Make (America) Great Again". NO, NO, NO, they are exactly the CON MAN that would have you believe that they are just the one who can make your country great again so that they will be given the Golden Opportunity to do just the opposite while you are looking on in wonder and total disbelief that your "saviour" is taking you and your beloved country down the toilet to Wrack and Ruin.

You look on in horror and bewilderment as your Democracy is stolen from you - slowly, slowly, step by stealthful step - Law by Law, Tradition by Tradition, Institution by Institution, Honor by Honor, Reputation by Reputation, Process by Process, Value by Value, Freedom by Freedom, Immigrant by Immigrant, Religion by Religion, Treaty by Treaty, Ally by Ally, Citizen by Citizen, Norm by Norm, Soul by Soul and Cherished Memories by Cherished Memories! THINK ABOUT IT! Just think back these very short 3 ½ years and count up what you have lost - essentially forever! Count up all the things that you used to believe in that has been normalized away from you - drip by drip! One of the biggest of these - and by far the most serious to you as an individual but far more importantly collectively is Truth - IS TRUTH! At no time has the adherence to truth been a partisan issue. All peoples universally declare allegiance to truth and value of truth. So look at what has been declared by one party in particular to be the new acceptable norm? 20,000 LIES in less than 1250 days in office! That's 16 LIES a day! There's absolutely nothing you can believe in. He's irrelevant!

114   OH MY GOD! Since June 1st, 2020 these United States have become so vulnerable to being - almost at the snap of a finger - an autocratic or possibly a totally Fascist country - that may be somehow tied to Russia in a non reversible way. Remember the first chapter? Yellow, Pinko Commie Lover? An almost 1000 page report just released by the Senate Intelligence Committee - clearly shows numerous direct connections to Putin's Russia during the campaign and possibly well since then. We know that the Resident has talked to Putin at least 5 times since late March and has a desire to have a private conversation with him again before the election. With the numerous suspicions from the news, the Mueller Report and now the Senate committee report - who in their right mind would allow such a meeting? Apparently the GOP lakeys would. During the campaign there were at least 272 contacts between the Campaign team and Russian linked operatives. The scary part now is the use of Military style operatives against the Civilian population - first on June 1st to clear a peaceful demonstration near the WH for a Bible PHOTO OP. and then for two months in Portland, OR and Seattle WA to quel "so called" violent demonstrations - that had been peaceful until the Thug, Jack storm troopers showed up. They wore no identification, insignias, name plates and apparently had no authorization to be there. That is a clear violation of the Posse Comitatus act of 1878. For all anyone knew, they could have been gun toting "white supremacists' ' in camo much as those who invaded the Michigan State Capitol in May 2020. Apparently there was no opposition to that insurrection. This all sets an ominous precedent for similar shenanigans that could be directed to disrupt, sway or defraud the Presidential election in November. Clearly one of the first tenants of the Constitution has been successfully breached many times - the Rule of Law. The next step is very likely tyranny of unlawful use of force, and authoritarianism. It must be stopped - NOW!

Made in United States
Troutdale, OR
03/29/2025